C000110508

SUCCESS IN THE STOCK MARKET

See the world through the eyes of a professional stock market investor

James Emanuel

Published by KDP

"An investment in knowledge pays the best interest."

When it comes to investing, nothing will pay off more than educating yourself - Do the necessary research, study, and analysis before making any investment decisions.

BENJAMIN FRANKLIN

CONTENTS

Title Page

Copyright

Epigraph

Prologue   1

Introduction   3

PART ONE   5

The magic formula   6

Strength of character   8

The biggest casino on earth   12

Skewing the odds   14

PART TWO   23

The father of value investing   24

Swimming with the turtles   30

Let me give you a tip   45

Far from the madding crowd   48

We're forever blowing bubbles   55

PART THREE   61

You get what you pay for, except at the stock-exchange   62

Boom and bust, ride it baby!   67

It's all about staying power   80

PART FOUR   83

To pe or not to pe, that is the question 84

Castles with a wide moat 88

Where to put the peg 95

Sales as a measure of value 97

The highs and lows of profit margins 101

Roe, roe, roe the boat to a better yield 105

Having a break down 117

PART FIVE 127

Share repurchases / stock buy-backs 128

Don't write me off just yet! 142

All that glitters is not gold 146

Debt, a friend or a foe? 169

Ebitda, da, da, da 178

Discount the discounted cash flow model 181

PART SIX 187

There is no one size fits all 188

Dividend policy 191

Timing is everything 196

The big test 201

It's all about the management 213

Qualitative analysis 224

Macro-economic considerations 234

Conclusion 241

Appendices 243

Glossary 249

Acknowledgement 263

About The Author 267

PROLOGUE

So you fancy yourself as a stock-market investor?

Why not? It looks glamorous in the movies.

Who wouldn't want to make lots of money, drive fast cars, eat at the best restaurants, travel the world in private jets and generally live the high-life?

Well I do not wish to burst your bubble, but unfortunately the reality is not Gordon Gekko in the 1987 film *Wall Street,* nor is it Jordan Belfort in the 2014 movie *The Wolf of Wall Street.*

Hollywood is in the business of dramatising everything. Entertaining, yes. A reflection of reality, no.

That having been said there are plenty of people who put their money to work in the stock market and who generate substantial returns as a result.

The key to success is simple - you need to understand what you are doing.

A statement of the obvious perhaps, but I can assure you that many people who choose to invest in the stock market are absolutely clueless.

No one would expect to be able to drive a car without first having taken driving lessons; nor to build a house without having learned the skills of construction. So why do so many people expect to be able to play in the financial markets without the correct knowledge or expertise?

Human psychology is a peculiar thing. I shall not attempt to justify it. Instead I offer this observation merely as an explanation of why so many people lose money when investing in shares.

There are a great many fools in this world!

I take comfort in the fact that you are reading this book in order to educate yourself and so you are evidently not one of those fools.

I anticipate that the world of stock market investing for you at the moment may be something of a mystery. Numbers that mean little or nothing at all.

You may feel as though you are groping around in the dark not knowing exactly what you hope to find.

If this is indeed the case then by the end of this book all of that will have changed. You will see the stock market through new eyes and with absolute clarity.

From darkness came light!

INTRODUCTION

May I begin by thanking you for choosing my book. Perhaps it was pure chance, or maybe you were recommended by a friend or a colleague. Either way I am confident that you will find it to be a good choice and hope that you will in turn recommend it to others.

There are a many self professed experts out there who write books with an alluring title such as *"How to trade the stock market and to retire at 40"* or *"How to become a stock market millionaire"*.

Bah! Humbug!

One of the sad realities is that these charlatans make money selling an impossible dream and many of these authors have never themselves practiced what they preach. Most are professional writers rather than traders and it would not surprise me to learn that most had never traded the stock market themselves.

Consider this, if an author of a book knew a formula which guaranteed success, then why is he not using that formula himself rather then attempting to forge a living by writing and selling books?

I have a rule in life which has never once let me down. If something appears too good to be true, then it is too good to be true.

And so, if you come across a book that professes to sell the impossible dream, use it as winter fuel by burning it when it gets cold in the winter. Do yourself a favour by not wasting time reading it!

My success in the field of investing is largely down to the greatest investors of all time who altruistically share their expertise with others.

I doubt that Benjamin Graham's motivation for writting his books *Security Analysis* and *The Intelligent Investor* was the accumulation of vast riches that come with textbook writing.

Similarly Warren Buffett has been happy to share his investing techniques for free with anyone who cares to read his Berkshire Hathaway annual Chairman's letter.

Graham and Buffett will feature heavily throughout this book.

PART ONE

Dipping a toe in the water

THE MAGIC FORMULA

Chapter One

I am sorry to disappoint you, but the honest truth about stock market investing is that there is no magic formula.

Every investor sets out to beat the market which is a fair and reasonable objective.

Indeed, if we are unable to beat the market we may be best advised to put our money in a tracker fund that emulates the performance of the market and so save ourselves a great deal of time and effort.

So beat the market we shall!

'Beat the market' in this context means over the long term. In the short term unprofitable companies may perform exceptionally well due to the irrational exuberance of speculators acquiring their shares.

Achieving a higher return than that offered by the market is referred to in market jargon as seeking *Alpha* (the Greek letter α) where Alpha is the excess return achieved over that of the market.

In economic terms we will only outperform the market by

seeking out good companies that will profitably grow the value of their businesses faster than the growth rate of the domestic economy as a whole. This is simple common sense.

However, be warned that investing in the stock market is a zero-sum game.

Because the market is comprised of all investors, the sum of the gains and losses of all investors will equal the overall market return for the corresponding period.

Ergo, for every investor that outperforms the market, there will be one or more offsetting investors who underperform by a like amount.

So the suggestion that there can be a magic formula, which by definition would work for everyone, is simply preposterous!

Is it a bad thing that there is no magic formula?

No, certainly not.

To the contrary it is a very good thing.

If a risk free money making algorithm existed then everyone would use it, price and value would never diverge and there would be no favourable investment opportunities to be had.

Instead, the market is full of inefficiencies which opens the door on many money making possibilities.

The question then becomes, how do I best find these trading opportunities and how do I capitalise upon them?

STRENGTH OF CHARACTER

Chapter Two

T he part that you may not want to hear is that making money from the stock market is all about discipline and a great deal of hard work.

Yes you may delegate that work to others, for a fee. This is what fund managers do for a living. The challenge then becomes finding a good fund manager (not as easy a task as it may sound).

So I shall assume that at this stage you wish to continue to manage your own investing. Why not?

First, forget any notion of getting rich quick. If you are exceptionally lucky you may strike gold by finding a share which explodes in value.

Amazon Inc. was such a share which would have seen a $50,000 investment in 2008 worth $2m today. A total gain of 3,900%. That is an astonishing average growth rate of 36% per year for 12 consecutive years. Said differently, the value of the investment more than doubled every two years with the benefit of compounded growth.

But even if you had invested in Amazon back in 2008, would you have ridden the wave for 12 years? Or would you have cashed-in early when the share had perhaps only doubled? Most amateur investors would have taken the latter course of action.

Do you have what it takes to move from an amateur's mind set to that of a professional investor?

Let us first test ourselves in order to understand whether we fully appreciate what it is that we are getting in to.

1. **Are you able to think in numbers?** It is not necessary to have a PhD in Astro-Physics, but if you struggled in basic high school mathematics then perhaps numbers are not your strong point.

2. **Do you have a genuine interest in businesses and how they operate?** If not, how do you hope to analyse company after company in order to find your next golden investment?

3. **Do you have the time to throughly research a business, its rivals and the industry generally in order to reach an informed decision about whether or not to invest your hard earned money?** If not, perhaps you would be best advised trusting your money to a high quality fund manager who will undertake this work on your behalf. There are plenty of exchange traded funds charging modest fees. One word of advice, if you decide to take this path, avoid passive funds and find a quality active fund manager (more on this later).

4. **Do you have the right temperament?** If you are an emotional person prone to panic when the market sentiment changes contrary to your interests then stock market investing may not be an appropriate occupation for you. Similarly, if you are over excitable and inclined to take profits too early then again you might want to rethink your ambition. You need to be confident and stoic. You must not become emotionally attached to

any individual trade – accept that some will be successful and some will fail. A 100% success rate is an unachievable aspiration. Even the best investors in the world experience failure approximately 30% - 40% of the time. This is a numbers game and if you are up more than 50% of the time then you are winning.

5. **Do you have sufficient levels of funds to invest?** This is important for two reasons. First, you need to be able to maintain a diverse portfolio of investments in order to manage risk (you do not want all of your eggs in one basket). Second, transaction costs for small sum investing undermine the viability of the enterprise. Imagine a flat brokerage fee of $7 per trade. If you invest only $100 then you are already down 7% in fees before you have started (and you will need to pay another similar fee when you sell). However, invest $10,000 and your transaction costs become a less significant 0.07%.

If you have satisfied yourself that you are ready to become a stock market investor then you must start to trade. There is no substitute for it. You must also make mistakes and learn from them. Making mistakes is part of trading. If you do not start trading using actual money - and enough money that it affects you when you win or lose - then you will never learn how to be a trader.

By analogy you could read any number of books describing perfectly how to drive a car, but none would prepare you to sit behind the wheel and to drive faultlessly on your first attempt. The only way to learn would be to get yourself in a car and to spend hours gaining practical experience on the road with a driving instructor by your side providing advice and guidance.

And so it is that this book should be used to supplement your practical trading experience. It contains the learnings of your author gathered over a 25 year career in the financial markets.

It is written to furnish you with invaluable advice and guidance which will speed up your practical learning, it will highlight the pitfalls to avoid and it will open your eyes to lessons learned by the many that trod the same path before you.

The book is full of interesting historical anecdotes interlaced with technical explanations broken down in layman's terms that are easily digested by a person with little or no experience of trading the stock market.

By the end of this book your perspective on the stock market ought to have shifted considerably, to the point that you will see the world of investing through entirely new eyes. The mist will have lifted and in its place will be clarity. Fear of the unknown will have been replaced by confidence.

And so, without further ado, allow me to take you by the hand and guide you on a journey into the wonderful world of stock market investing.

THE BIGGEST CASINO ON EARTH

Chapter Three

Many people argue that the stock market is the world's largest casino, a game of chance.

I certainly do not share that view. The stock market is no game.

Investing in companies is a serious business that requires time, skill and expertise.

There is a fundamental difference between a gambler and an investor as I shall go on to explain in this chapter with reference to a few interesting historical anecdotes.

First, allow me to ask you, the reader, a rhetorical question. Allow yourself a few moments to consider the question, and to answer it in your own mind, before reading on.

If I were to flip a fair coin and offer you the opportunity to speculate on either a "heads" or a "tails" outcome - I would pay you one dollar should you be correct, but you would pay me one dollar if you are wrong - would you accept those terms?

A gambler would certainly do it because it is a fair bet and he is only interested in making a quick buck in the very short term, perhaps also enjoying the rush of adrenalin brought about by the excitement of the bet.

An investor, on the other hand, would not be interested in such a proposal. This is because the chances of success are not skewed in his favour. He is not interested in making fast money - he is only concerned with deploying a strategy over the longer term which will reward his investment (time and capital) with a worthwhile return.

Said differently, the investor knows that if he accepts this challenge 100 times or more then he will be successful 50% of the time and unsuccessful the other 50% of the time. His wins will be offset by his losses and his time will have been entirely wasted with no net financial gain.

So now I hope that you are beginning to understand the difference between a gambler and an investor. On the same basis I would argue that a professional stock market investor cannot be considered a gambler and so by extension, the stock market cannot be classified as a casino.

The customers of a casino are all gamblers who speculate their hard earned money in the knowledge that the odds of winning are always against them. I consider these people to be either fools intent on losing money or else criminals attempting to launder dirty money!

The owner of a casino, on the other hand, is a canny investor who always wins because the odds are constantly skewed in his favour.

I sincerely hope that you have an investors mindset rather than that of a gambler. If not, then you may be best advised to stop reading now because you may well be a lost cause.

◆ ◆ ◆

SKEWING THE ODDS

Chapter Four

We are able to learn a great deal from history and so allow me to take you on a journey back in time.

The year was 1650 and the place was Paris, France.

A man known as the Chevalier de Mere, a smart fellow, sought to generate an income for himself by betting with the aristocracy while skewing the odds of the game in his favour.

These were the days prior to probability theory and so the Chevalier was certainly ahead of his time.

In a letter to the great mathematician, Blaise Pascal, the Chevalier boasted, *"I have discovered in mathematics things so rare that the most learned of ancient times have never thought of them..."*

The Chevalier knew that the chance of throwing a six on a die is one in six (16.7%). He had further calculated, correctly, that the probability of throwing a six with a single die rises to just above 50% with four throws (the actual probability is 51.8%).

Accordingly, in the gentlemen's clubs that he would frequent he would wager that he will roll a six in four rolls of a fair die. If he succeeded then he would win a gold coin, but if he failed then he would pay his opponent a gold coin (an even money bet).

The strategy was to win a tiny amount on a large number of games in contrast to betting his entire Chateau on a single roll.

It was of critical importance that the odds were only slightly skewed in his favour. In every 100 games he would lose an average of 48 times.

To his opponents, not themselves expert in mathematics, the game looked fair and not keeping a tally of wins versus losses it appeared that both players had an even chance of success.

Additionally, the Chevalier would play a small number of games with a multitude of players so that some of his opponents would prosper which resulted in no shortage of people willing to challenge the Chevalier to a few games.

Since the Chevalier had the odds skewed in his favour, the large number of games that he played in total meant that he was guaranteed to profit. There was in fact no risk.

The plan required the deployment of a large amount of capital because a six may fail to appear for many roles of the die before appearing more frequently, but he was convinced that over the long term he would win more than he lost and so generate a handsome return on the capital that he had invested.

The principal is exactly the same as that deployed by Casinos today. The odds of every game are skewed in favour of the house and against the gamblers. More people will lose than will win and so the Casino makes a risk free profit from its enterprise.

Consider the Roulette wheel for example. The game, and the name, also have their roots in France and date back to the late 1790s (probably inspired by the antics of the Chevalier).

In fact, Blaise Pascal, confidant of the Chevalier, has often been attributed with the accolade of introducing the game to the world.

On a Roulette wheel there are 18 black numbers, 18 red numbers and a green zero. The green zero means that there is a 51.4% probability that the casino wins and only a 48.6% chance that the gambler will win.

Does that sound familiar?

In the days of the Chevalier his opponents could be forgiven for taking an even money bet with odds that were skewed against them on the basis that they believed the chances to be even and fair.

Those who frequent casinos today have no such excuse. It is an enigma to me how so many people accept unfavourable terms and squander their money on a lost cause.

In any event, back to our friend the Chevalier. He was so overwhelmed with the success of his strategy that he became a little too confident in his own ability. He tried to invent variations of the game in order to maintain the intrigue of prospective opponents.

One such variation, also with dice, involved betting that *sonnez* (the French term for double-six) would appear in 24 throws of a pair of dice.

The Chevalier had calculated, as before, that the odds were once again in his favour, although he was wrong on this occasion.

Again he applied a large amount of capital to this new strategy over a great many games in the mistaken belief that the long term average would favour his purse. However, this time he lost a fortune.

The probability of success in 24 throws of a pair of dice was only 49.14%. The odds were against the Chevalier. Had he bet on 25 throws, where the probability of throwing a double-six is 50.55% he would have prospered. Such are the narrow margins between success and failure!

If you are interested in the mathematics behind the games played by the Chevalier then please refer to Appendix One.

The Chevalier almost bankrupted himself and, frustrated, wrote to Blaise Pascal seeking a better mathematical brain than his own to work out what had gone so terribly wrong.

Pascal worked with Pierre de Fermat, another outstanding French mathematician, to solve the problem encountered by the Chevalier. The outcome, published in 1654 in correspondence, was a pivotal moment in the history of mathematics and the development of the theory of probability as we know it today.

There are lessons to be learned here when it comes to calculating risk which may be applied by way of analogy to a stock market investor. These may be summed up as follows:

- Do not expect every risk taken (every investment) to yield a positive outcome. Expect some investments to result in a loss.

- View investing holistically as a large collection of risks which, if the odds are properly skewed in your favour, will yield a positive net outcome.

- Mismanaging risk so that the odds are even remotely against you will result in disastrous consequences.

We do not leave our historical French friends there. Indeed, there is more that they are able to teach us.

Shortly afterwards Pascal became very religious. The reason for this is rooted in probability theory and once again has lessons for us as stock market investors.

In 1654 Pascal abandoned mathematics and physics, he sold all of his possessions save for religious books and began to live a more pious life. He dropped all of his friends and took up residence in the monastery of Port-Royal in Paris.

Why such a dramatic change?

The answer may be discovered in his diary, written while living a monastic life at Port-Royal.

We discover that his religious deliberations were pondered with his outstanding mathematical mind which never ceased to play with the concept of probability.

Most well known is what has now become known as Pascal's Wager:

> *"God is, or he is not. Which way should we incline?"*
> *Blaise Pascal*

Pascal postulates there is no way to reach a definitive answer by reason alone. He argues that one might toss a coin: heads, God is; tails, God is not. But this did not sit easily in his mind. One could not allow chance to determine a solution to such a question.

Philosophically Pascal concluded that the matter is absolutely binary: a person may either believe or not believe. The person who believes will live a spiritual devout life adhering to the rules of his religion. The person who decides not to live a God-fearing religious life is essentially wagering that God is not.

He goes further to consider the consequences of both courses of action. If God is not, whether you lead your life piously or sinfully is immaterial. However, if God is, and you bet against his existence by refusing to live a life of piety then you run the risk of eternal damnation.

It was thus clear to Pascal that the downside of betting against God and being wrong was huge, while the downside of believing in God and being wrong was immaterial. To Pascal it was obvious which way he would live the remainder of his life.

And therein is an important lesson for the stock market investor. Every investment decision is binary: To invest or not to invest. The determination is often best made by considering the risks or consequences of being wrong.

Investing is, ultimately, an exercise of balancing risk versus reward. This was something that the Chevalier de Mere fully understood although something that he miscalculated to his great cost.

What might we learn from our French friends?

•	Always consider the materiality of the downside risk before making any investment decision. What are the worst consequences if you get it wrong?

•	Do not invest in haste. Take your time to analyse an investment, to understand it and to balance risk versus reward. Skew the odds in your favour.

•	Perhaps if the Chevalier had sought the counsel of Pascal prior to gambling away all of his money, rather than afterwards, he may have died a happier man. So, do not be afraid to ask questions and to seek the views and opinions of others before making a decision.

So now is the time to bid farewell to Paris and to travel across the English Channel to historic London.

A London casino owner by the name of John Henry Martindale developed what is now known as the Martingale strategy otherwise known as the doubling strategy. (Martindale, for whatever reason, evolved into Martingale over time).

The concept is quite simple, you place your bet on an even money bet. After every loss you double your stake and bet again and you keep on doing that until such time as you win. The first win will recover all previous losses, plus give you a profit equal to your original bet. At this point you start all over again with your original bet, which you double again until your next win.

So on the toss of a coin you may bet one coin on "heads". If successful you win one coin, if not then you lose one coin.

On the assumption that you lose your first bet, the second bet will be for two coins on the same basis. If successful you win two coins, but since you lost one coin on the first bet your net winnings will only ever be one coin.

It may in fact take many flips of the coin before your first win but whenever you are successful your winnings will always be only one coin more than all of your previous losses.

It sounds very much like a guaranteed winning strategy, but here is the rub. As a direct result of doubling on each successive bet the Martingale approach deploys vast amounts of capital. For example, if it takes you eight flips of a coin before you win then you are betting 128 coins in order to win a single coin!

So yet again, history is able to teach the stock market investor an invaluable lesson.

Making a financial gain is not in itself sufficient justification for the investment. The return on investment must be calculated with reference to both the capital utilised, and indeed the time expended, in generating that financial gain.

As a point of pure curiosity to wrap up this chapter, you may be interested to learn that in 1891 a man by the name of Charles De Ville Wells is credited with having deployed the Martingale technique in a casino in Monte Carlo to great success. He is credited with "breaking the bank of Monte Carlo" by winning one million francs (there is a movie and a book that dramatises the story).

After that time casinos introduced maximum bets to frustrate anyone attempting to use the Martingale system.

PART TWO

Wading in the shallow end

THE FATHER OF VALUE INVESTING

Chapter Five

O ne of the greatest stock market investors of all time, considered the father of value investing, is a gentleman named Benjamin Graham.

He was born in London in 1894 but his family emigrated to the US while he was still a baby. Unfortunately, Graham's father died when he was only seven years of age and his family drifted from prosperity into poverty. His mother turned the family home into a boarding house and sought to enhance her income by speculating on shares. Tragedy struck the family again when the stock market crashed in 1907 and his mother lost what little she had.

It is said that early experiences in life are character building and so it was with Graham. He later became one of he most successful stock market investors of all time and developed a unique philosophy on the differences between speculation and investing which would guide his success.

For further reading please see Security Analysis, a book written by Benjamin Graham, first edition was published in 1934, which laid the intellectual foundation for what would later be called value investing. The most recent edition has a foreword from

Warren Buffett.

Warren Buffett, also known as the sage of Omaha, is a modern day investment genius but know this - Buffet learned his trade working for Benjamin Graham.

Graham became an investment fund manager having established the Graham Newman Corp with a friend Jerome Newman.

By the time that he retired in 1956 he had achieved an average annual growth rate of 20% gross (17% after deduction of his fees) which was twice the return of the market in the same period. At this rate the value of funds under his management doubled once every three-and-a-half years and the compounded growth that he achieved for his investors from 1933 to his retirement in 1956 was a staggering 3700%.

At the centre of Graham's trading philosophy was a determination to secure high returns combined with relatively low risk. We refer to this now as value investing.

Risk versus reward analysis is critical to being successful.

If you consider the coin flip analogy once again then you will appreciate that the risk and reward are perfectly balanced - 50% of the flips you will lose versus 50% that you will win.

This would not have met the Graham threshold for a viable investment opportunity and rightly so. He wanted the risk to be lower than 50% and the reward to be more than 50%.

He termed the difference between risk and reward as his margin of safety and this principle governed his investment decisions throughout his career.

An investment with no margin of safety he considered to be

pure speculation and foolhardy.

> *"When you build a bridge, you insist that it can carry 30,000 pounds, but you only drive 10,000 pound trucks across it. You require a margin of safety, and rightly so."*
> *Warren Buffett*

That same principle works in investing.

Attempting to ascribe a precise valuation to a company is impossible and so, in fact, foolish. We have no way of knowing what the future will bring in terms of prosperity or frustration for the company in question. Working with a range of possibilities is therefore the only approach.

So, utilising a margin of safety means only buying shares in a company when the price is substantially lower than the range of possibilities that you have ascribed to the future value of that company. This allows for human error, bad luck, or extreme volatility in a complex, unpredictable and rapidly changing world.

Safety was key to preserving the integrity of Graham's fund and growing the value of the equity that he held on behalf of those that trusted him with their money. Said differently, he laid solid foundations on which he was able to build a fortune while most stock market players build their houses on sand!

Graham was one for undertaking detailed analysis prior to embarking on any investment. The question was always one of value against price.

A particular share may be considered as an investment at one price, while the same share would be speculative at a higher price.

Graham believed that there was no reliable way of making money easily or quickly. He often warned against over exuberance: *'greed and unfounded optimism'* which he said merely encouraged people to abandon the basic common sense principles of investing.

> " ... the psychology of the speculator...he is most optimistic when prices are highest and most despondent when they are at bottom...For this reason, training in speculation, however intelligent and thorough, is likely to prove a misfortune to the individual, since it may lead him into market activities which, starting in most cases with small successes, almost invariably end in major disaster."
> Benjamin Graham

Graham instead followed a safety first approach, not aiming for unreasonably high returns but concentrating on sound investment principles.

While others experienced the euphoria of booms and the misery of busts, Graham's cautious but structured approach allowed him to outperform the market year after year.

Many people tend not to understand the fundamentals of value investing but instead put their money in the most well known companies of the day which become ever more overvalued as each new wave of investors pumps money blindly into its shares.

Apple became the first company with a market price of over 1 trillion US dollars on this basis – was it worth $1 trillion dollars in value at that time or were investors paying an unreasonable premium?

Well, after breaching the $1 trillion dollar mark in August 2018, Apple stock subsequently tumbled 31% over the four months that followed and by December of that same year had a market capitalisation of 'only' $692 billion dollars.

These businesses may be performing well but where they are over priced they offer no value. Not only is their anticipated future success already included in the price, which means limited or no upside in the investment, but they carry a very high degree of downside risk.

The risk versus reward profile simply does not work.

By way of another example, from 1995 to 2000 the company Texas Instruments increased its earnings by a factor of ten but over the same period so many investors bought its shares that the market capitalisation expanded by 55 times.

As the share price rose so rapidly even more investors jumped on the band-wagon looking for a piece of the action. This surge of demand caused the price to run far ahead of the underlying value of the company.

In fact the share price grew so rapidly over this short period of time that there were multiple 2-for-1 stock splits to keep the shares affordable for the average investor.

Ultimately, the company commanded such a premium that despite having demonstrated exceptional earnings growth, between 2000 and 2002 the price corrected and fell 80% as the chart below demonstrates.

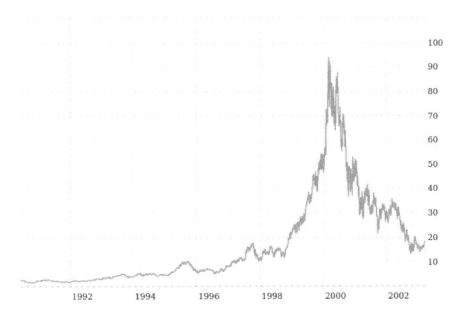

Benjamin Graham's philosophy was one of safety first. If a good company was mis-priced relative to it intrinsic value then he argued that there was very little further downside in the investment. If the company appeared to be of good quality but under-priced then there would be more than a reasonable chance for a price shift to the upside and so the odds of success were skewed in his favour. This he termed intelligent investing.

Texas Instruments would not have met Benjamin Graham's criteria for being a value investment and so he would have avoided the huge losses that so many others in the stock market suffered.

SWIMMING WITH THE TURTLES

Chapter Six

T he most important aspects of successful stock market trading are confidence, consistency, and discipline.

Discipline is of critical importance. Understand the rules of the game and stick to them religiously.

Traders who want to be successful will figure out a way to gain enough confidence in their own rules of trading to be able to apply them consistently.

Rules that you cannot, or will not, follow are of absolutely no use.

So, what are these rules?

Allow me to answer that question by telling you a fascinating true story.

The year was 1983 and two financial market traders were having a disagreement over a beer in Chicago. Their names were Richard Dennis, a very successful commodities trader, and Bill Eckhardt.

The dispute centred on whether great traders were the product of nature or nurture. The question was whether a person could be taught to be a good trader or whether it was some form of innate skill that some people were born with.

Dennis believed that he could teach people to become great traders. Eckhardt thought that genetics and aptitude were the determining factors.

The matter led to the friends making a bet with each other which would be determined by way of an experiment.

Dennis advertised in the Wall Street Journal and the New York Times newspapers which subsequently led ot the recruitment of thirteen people whom had never traded before.

The trainees came from all walks of life, but none had been involved in financial markets previously.

Dennis nicknamed the group "the Turtles" because Dennis said that he would grow traders just like they grow turtles in Singapore.

He coached them for a month or two and each Turtle was given a trading account with a cash balance to trade.

The money, several million dollars in total, was provided by Dennis who had himself accumulated a great deal of wealth from trading activities. He was confident in his own ability to coach the Turtles sufficiently well to grow the money he had invested in them.

Needless to say Dennis won the bet. The Turtle Traders became the most famous experiment in trading history. According to Russell Sands, a former Turtle Trader, as a group the two classes of Turtles that Dennis personally trained earned more than $175 million in only five years.

It should be noted that the Turtles were trading futures contracts on the US commodity exchanges in New York and Chicago, but most of the principles applied by them are equally valid when trading equities on the stock market.

How did they do it?

The system covered every aspect of managing a trading position and left virtually no decision to the subjective whims of the trader.

Know this, there is no perfect system that will allow a trader to win on every investment he makes. Remember our friend the Chevalier de Mere from earlier in the book. Trading is about skewing the odds in your favour and winning more than you lose so that on average you are up.

There will always be sustained periods of losses and this is the time when emotions must be kept in check. Stick to your system and you will eventually prevail.

Although the Turtle system worked well it was far from plain sailing. There were periods of losses, for example the day after the October 1987 Stock market crash when the U.S. Federal Reserve lowered interest rates aggressively the Turtles saw their account equity fall by over 20% in a single day. But they had confidence in their system, stuck rigidly to the rules, and they had far more good days than bad days.

In some years their equity grew by 80% or more.

By analogy, the Chevalier had formulated rules that were working for him. But over confidence led him to change the rules of his own game which all but bankrupted him. The moral of the story is that there is no need to fix something that is not broken. If your rules work, do not deviate from them.

So, you need to devise a complete trading system that allows you to decide the following:

1. Markets - What to buy

2. Position Sizing – How much to buy

3. Entries – When to buy

4. Managing what you have bought

5. Exits – when to get out of a winning positions

6. Tactics – How to buy or sell

Let us deal with each in turn.

1. Markets - What to buy

This is a choice that you need to make at the outset.

You want to focus on a particular market rather than being a Jack of all trades and master of none.

Know your market so that you are able to recognise good buying and selling opportunities.

If you are focused on the stock market rather than perhaps commodity markets or foreign exchange markets then you need to ask yourself if you feel that you ought to specialise further.

Perhaps you might want to invest in tecnology stocks, or pharmaceutical companies, or oil and gas businesses. This is a choice that only you can make.

I would urge you to play in several market sectors rather than only one as this gives you the protection of diversification. For example, you do not want to be exposed to only oil stocks and then find that OPEC makes a surprise decision that sinks your entire portfolio. However, be consistent and stick to markets that you know and understand rather than flitting around.

Benjamin Graham coined the phrase Enterprise Investing to describe someone who specialises in a particular type of industry and so gains a depth of knowledge and understanding that will give him an edge over other investors.

In such circumstances he advocated a lower level of diversification on the basis that it is better to concentrate on businesses that you have a high degree of certainty will perform very well, rather than holding a range of mediocre companies merely for diversification's sake. He did warn, however, that to succeed as an expert in a particular field would require viewing investing as a full time enterprise rather than just as a part time hobby.

Ultimately you will need to decide which level of diversification works best for you.

On the subject of stock diversification in your portfolio, *Beta* (the Greek letter β) is an interesting financial measure. See Appendix 3 for the Beta coefficient formula, although you can avoid the maths as you should be able to find the Beta coefficient for most shares pre-calculated on a multitude of financial websites.

Beta measures how correlated an individual stock price is to the broader stock market index. If the stock price follows the index perfectly then it has a Beta of one. If the stock price moves in the opposite direction to the index then it is inversely correlated and so will have a Beta of minus one. A Beta of more than one means that the stock exaggerates the movements of the index, and so on and so forth.

Beta allows you to calculate the likely volatility of your portfolio as a whole. First calculate your weighted average Beta across all stocks in your portfolio. If your portfolio has a high Beta you might like to purchase some negative or low Beta stocks in order to bring the average down, and vice versa. This is all about portfolio management.

A zero Beta portfolio, theoretically a market volatility risk neutral state of affairs, will in aggregate be unaffected by the volatility of the underlying market.

On the subject of diversification, as you become more adept at picking winners you will have the confidence to reduce the number of holdings in your portfolio.

Warren Buffett's top five holdings have accounted for an average of 73% of his portfolio over the last 25 years. In fact, at the end of 1999 Berkshire Hathaway had 70% of its multi-billion dollar investment fund in only four companies!

> *"I cannot understand why an investor ... elects to put money into a business that is his 20th favorite [company] rather than simply adding that money to his top choices." Warren Buffett*

This leads nicely to the next part of the trading system jigsaw puzzle – that of position sizing.

2. Position Sizing - How much to buy

It cannot be overstated how important this decision is. Essentially this is about money management.

The Turtles traded futures contracts on various commodities together with interest rates. The trading techniques that they used is markedly different from the techniques required for equity investing. As such the volatility mechanisms used by the Turtles to determine the size of each position together with the Donchian breakout trade entry system that they favoured are not relevant for you and so beyond the scope of this book. However, the principle remains the same as I shall go on to explain.

You will be familiar with the proverb of not putting all of your eggs in one basket. Diversification is important as a means of mitigating risk. It is an attempt to spread risk across many investments and to increase the opportunity for profit by increasing the opportunities for catching successful trades.

With reference once again to the Chevalier de Mere, he would place many small bets because he had no idea which rolls of the dice would be winners and which would be losers. Had he bet everything on a single roll of the die his system would not have worked.

As a rule I would urge you to not put anymore than 3% of your investment fund in any single investment. If you were to follow this rule then you would always have a portfolio of at least 33 different investments and if any one should underperform, or indeed fail completely, then the materiality of your loss on the entire fund will be curtailed.

To properly diversify requires making similar if not identical bets on many different investments. However, the subsequent scaling of those positions helps to magnify gains and mitigate losses – see (4) below. This is a key rule and one that needs to be adhered to. It is actually the opposite of what most amateur investors do (which is why the Turtles succeeded and most amateur investors fail).

3. Entries - When to buy

In essence, if your analysis tells you that the market price is lower than the intrinsic value of the share that you are buying then you have a greater chance of price catching up with value than you do of the price weakening further.

Again, this is about skewing the odds in your favour.

This is generally an assessment of price against value (more on this later).

4. Managing what you have bought?

A trader needs to know when to get out of a losing position. Traders who do not abandon erroneous decisions by cutting their losses relatively early will not be successful in the long term.

In respect of losing positions an amateur investor will usually hold the position in the hope that the price will bounce back thereby allowing him to mitigate the loss.

For most people, it is far easier to cling to the hope that a losing trade will turn around than it is to accept the loss, admit that the trade did not work out and to move on.

In respect of winning positions an amateur is usually anxious to crystalise his gain quickly, perhaps for fear that the price may subsequently drop.

And so, it is a well known fact that most amateur investors will take profit too early and will hold on to losses for too long.

The result of this disasterous strategy is that small profits are taken and big losses are sustained, resulting in net losses over-all.

To make matters worse, many amateur investors will "double down" on a loss in a misguided attempt to recover. So for example, buying an investment at $1.00 and finding the price slipping back to $0.80 the amateur will buy more at the lower price to bring his average entry price down to $0.90 – in his mind the market only needs to recover ten cents rather than the full twenty cents in order to wipe out his loss. What he fails to understand is that the price momentum is to the downside and if the investment slips further, perhaps to $0.60, he has in fact multiplied his losses. Please do not make this very common mistake. Have this as one of your hard and fast trading rules.

It is not just amateurs that make this mistake. Financial institutions including Barings bank and Long-term Capital Management collapsed because professional traders refused to cut their losses which subsequently grew out of control.

It is also important not to set the threshold at which you will cut your losses too close to the entry price. Prices never go straight up; therefore it is necessary to let the prices go against you if you are going to ride a trend.

Early in a trend this can often mean watching a 20% profit fade to a small loss. In the middle of a trend, it might mean watching a profit of 80% being cut in half. If the fundamental reason for entering the trade is still valid there is no need to stop out these trades.

The time to cut your loss is when your premise for having entered the trade turns out to be flawed. Said differently, where you discover that you had made a fundamental mistake in your analysis.

In the absence of a sound basis for having entered into the trade, there is certainly no reason for holding on to it.

There is also the opportunity cost of not putting your capital to better use elsewhere. Why hold on to a 15% loss for a year or two hoping for a recovery when that money could be invested in a better company that may enable you to generate a 50% gain?

The most important thing about cutting your losses is to have predefined the point below the entry price where you will stop your losses.

Make this decision before you enter a trade.

If the market moves to your threshold then you must get out, no exceptions, no hesitation, every single time. Wavering from this method will eventually result in disaster.

On the trading floors of London and New York the traders amend the words of the Cat Stevens song *The First Cut is the Deepest* when they sing *"The first cut is the cheapest."* Cut your mistakes early because that ensures that losses remain small and manageable.

By contrast the approach of the Turtle Traders was diametrically opposite to that of the foolish amateur.

They would take a loss early, accepting that not every trading decision will be a winner.

However, if the Turtles found themselves in a winning trade they would scale up by incrementally adding to the trade up to three times. So they might buy at $1.00, buy again at $1.10, once more at $1.20 and a final trade at $1.30. If that winning trade continued to move higher then their winnings were multiplied by a factor of four! So instead of the amateur doubling down, the Turtles would quadruple up.

There is an old saying that: "you can never go broke taking a profit." A professional investor would not agree with this statement. Getting out of winning positions too early is one of the most common mistakes when trading.

It is all about skewing your odds of success. If you ride your profits and multiply them up, while cutting your losses early then the odds are skewed very much in your favour.

Most of the profits that the Turtle Traders made in any given year might only come from a small number of large winning trades. Ergo, if a multiplier trade was missed this could greatly affect the returns for the year.

On the subject of holding on to winners, good companies that have a niche in their industry, which are well managed and which allocate capital properly will grow and grow and grow.

Just think of the trajectory of Microsoft in the period from 1986 to 2020 – the best strategy would have been to hold these shares and to benefit from compounded growth year on year. A $1,000 investment in Microsoft on the day of its initial public offering (IPO) on 13th March 1986, would be worth more than $1.6 million today (includes price appreciation plus dividends). Now imagine having adopted the Turtle approach of scaling into the trade – the quadruple effect would have seen that investment being worth $6.4 million today!

Warren Buffett adopts a similar approach to investing. He has held shares in companies including Coca-Cola, Wells Fargo Bank and American Express for thirty years and has over time increased his stake in these winning companies.

Every time the Turtles scaled into a winning trade they would adjust their stop-loss upward relative to the level of the most recent trade. In this way the trade may be exited at a price below the last trade of the series but above the entry of the earliest trade. This helped provide the full affect of the multiplier for as long as the market moved in their favour, but lessened the impact of the multiplier in the event that there should be a fundamental change requiring a premature exit.

If the Turtles made four times the amount on a winning trade as they lost on a losing trade then they would only need to win one out of every four trades to be profitable – and if more than three out of every four trades turn sour then there is something seriously wrong with your stock picking analysis!

5. Exits - When to get out of a winning position

Many "trading systems" that are offered as complete trading systems do not specifically address the exit of winning positions. Yet the question of when to get out of a winning position is crucial to the profitability of the system. Any trading system that does not address the exit of winning positions is not a complete trading system.

Bear in mind that the Turtle Traders were concerned with futures and derivatives contracts. These are entirely different in nature to ownership of a share in a company.

In particular, futures and derivatives trading is, by its very nature, short term. A futures contract to expire next September for example only has a finite life - said differently, there is no buy and hold for the long term. Additionally, futures and derivatives trading is highly geared and requires capital to meet periodic margin calls. As such there is a material cost of carry which would make it uneconomic to hold these instruments for the long term.

By contrast equities are bearer securities which are bought with cash and so can be held indefinitely with no cost of carry, save for opportunity cost. Additionally, an equity in a good company should benefit from compounded growth on retained earnings and so shares possess a unique quality absent from other financial assets.

With investments in equities the exit is usually determined by one of three factors.

(a) Where the price runs too far ahead of your deemed intrinsic value of the share – in such a case it is often wise to take a profit. After all, if the share price has run ahead of valuation then the price will either stagnate until the value catches up with the price or else the price will fall back in line with intrinsic value. If the latter then you may have an opportunity to buy the share back at a lower price.

(b) Where the return on the share drops to a level where a better return may be had elsewhere. Said differently, a situation that lends itself to the reallocation of investment capital.

(c) Where there has been a fundamental change in the business or the industry that erodes the underlying competitive advantage that the company once had. This may be new technology, changes in government policy, a new less competent executive team or any other number of factors.

The great investors believe in selecting investments wisely and holding for the long term, or even indefinitely.

Ben Graham observed the folly of a traditional stock market investor as captured by the following quote.

> *"A rigid observance of old-time canons of common-stock investment would have dictated the sale of one's holdings at a substantial profit very early in the upswing and a heroic abstinence from further participation in the market until at some point ... when prices were again attractive in relation to earnings and other analytical factors." Benjamin Graham*

Graham knew that taking profit too early was foolhardy. He recognised the value of compounded growth over the long term. He also understood the opportunity cost that is the loss of compounded growth during periods of abstinence from the market.

Indeed, Warren Buffett is a buy and hold investor regardless of changes in market sentiment and price from time-to-time.

> *"Regardless of price, we have no interest at all in selling any good businesses that Berkshire owns." Warren Buffett*

The comment was made in relation to businesses owned entirely by Berkshire Hathaway rather than to marketable securities, but Buffett follows a similar approach for shares that he buys. As mentioned earlier in this chapter Buffett bought Coca-

Cola shares 1988, Wells Fargo shares in 1990 and American Express shares in 1993. Thirty years later he is still holding them. In fact he has added to alll of these positions over time, an active example of the multiplier affect discussed above.

6. Tactics - How to buy or sell

Once a buy signal has been triggered, tactical considerations regarding the mechanics of execution become important. This is especially true for larger accounts or for trading in less liquid stock, where the entry and exit of positions can result in significant adverse price movements.

However, even for a person trading smaller quantities it is important to determine whether to place a limit order at a specified price, or whether to give the broker discretion to execute the deal on your behalf at the best price that he can find in the market.

A limit order will provide you with more control over the execution price, but there may be an opportunity cost in terms of the time that is spent waiting for the market to reach your pre-defined entry target price. In fact, in a fast moving market the price may move further away from you resulting in you missing the trade altogether. So sometimes it would be better to bite the bullet and trade at market price immediately.

Note also that the decision as to whether you place a market order or a limit order will also turn on the liquidity of the asset being traded. Illiquid assets have a wide bid/offer spread and a market order will require you crossing that spread which may not be at all desirable. When the spread is wide a limit order is your best option. The bid/offer spread is effectively a transaction cost – you will invariably cross the spread one way when entering a trade and then cross the spread the other way when exiting the position, ergo a 2.5% spread will result in up to 5% being wiped off your profit. Liquid stocks, which are those with a constant high volume of buyers and sellers, have a narrow bid/offer spread (a small fraction of one percent) which is enormously advantageous to the trader.

The lesson to be learned from this part of the book is not only to formulate your own trading system rules, but to adhere to them religiously. You will need confidence in the rules or else you will abandon them when the market turns against you – which it inevitably will from time to time. That level of confidence will only come from knowing the rules intimately and understanding their reason for being. It is simply no good blindly adopting someone else's rules.

> *"I always say that you could publish my trading rules in the newspaper and no one would follow them. The key is consistency and discipline. Almost anybody can make up a list of rules that are 80% as good as what we taught our people. What they couldn't do is give them the confidence to stick to those rules even when things are going bad."*
> *Richard Dennis, instructor to the Turtle Traders*

You can break the rules and get away with it occasionally but eventually the rules will break you for not respecting them.

LET ME GIVE YOU A TIP

Chapter Seven

---

n investor must have faith in his or her own methodology for selecting good investments.

Ignore tips being passed around the office or amongst friends - buying a good luck story is like building a house on sand.

Instead you want to build your investment portfolio on solid foundations – facts and figures.

Additionally, as you will now have discovered, investing is a numbers game. It is about rolling the dice hundreds of times and ensuring that you win more than you lose – said differently, it is about investing in a diverse and well structured portfolio where the wins will inevitably outnumber the losses.

But there will be losses, there is no getting away from it. It is all a part of the game. So the next time someone you know announces a hot share tip and you see others investing their life savings on what they believe to be a sure thing (putting all of their eggs in one basket), you will smile knowingly to yourself and walk away.

Also disregard hot tips in the newspapers, on the internet or on

TV. Remember that the people behind these tips are not traders - they generally have no clue but are instead paid to take a view.

Even the analysts at the broking firms or big banks should be disregarded. They are not paid to be right, they are in fact paid to be less wrong than their competitors. This is why analysts constantly revise their share price targets incrementally in response to small revisions of other analysts.

Analysts at the brokerage firms are only concerned about keeping their job and so work on the basis that it is safer to stick with the crowd. As the illustrious economist John Maynard Keynes used to say, it is better to be vaguely right than to be being precisely wrong.

In any event banks and brokers are in the business of selling products to the public, and so tend towards optimism and away from reality. Said differently, bullish pronouncements are good for business.

It is absurd that anyone should think that market forecasting by pundits could lead to sustainable returns on investment. If the forecaster was confident in his own predictions he would be investing rather than commentating!

Investors who invest on the basis of hot tips, forecasts and recommendations of others may just as well gamble on red or black in a game of Roulette based on someone else's prediction of the outcome of the next spin of the wheel.

Even if a forecaster happens to be correct, by the time that you have read his opinion so too have thousands of other investors and the news will invariably already be in the price.

Even where the favourable information flows directly from the company itself, most public companies engage in the usual practice of providing "earnings guidance" or other information of value to analysts and large shareholders ahead of regular shareholders and the general public. By the time that you receive the news it will be too late as others will have capitalised on the opportunity a long time ahead of you.

Accordingly, as a good investor you will need to spot an investment opportunity yourself and most importantly, ahead of the crowd.

When the market eventually spots the opportunity the price will tend towards fair value and you will become the beneficiary of your own analysis by watching the value of your investment grow.

Long story short, do not follow the crowd. Which leads nicely to the next chapter.

FAR FROM THE MADDING CROWD

Chapter Eight

T here are many different category of stock market player but two prevalent types are the value based investor and the momentum oriented speculator.

The latter type is of the belief that because something increased in value yesterday, it will do so again today, and the next day and so on.

In the clothing industry people tend to follow the crowd, that is after all the essence of fashion. However, in the investment world, following the crowd is a disasterous approach.

Unfashionable companies often decline in value for a period to the extent that they become decidedly cheap. These will rise back towards fair value in time.

Similarly, stocks with a spectacular historic performance will invariably fall off their pedestals as rivals enter the market, technology changes occur or some other extraneous factor impedes their future growth.

By way of example, in the 1960s there were a group of blue chip companies known as the Nifty Fifty. Back then, this group of 50 large, good quality companies like General Electric and Polaroid were rated at anything up to 100 times earnings as investors poured in regardless of price - much like Facebook, Tesla and Netflix today. Eventually the wheels fell off when the market came to its senses and a stock market crash caused a long overdue price correction. When the S&P500, a US stock market index, fell by 39% between 1973-74, the Nifty Fifty fell by a whopping 47%. It took investors in these stocks a decade to recoup their losses and they never caught up with the broad market.

More particularly some of these darlings of yesteryear eventually went out of business, Polariod being a case in point. Polaroid employed 21,000 people at its peak, had turnover of $3 billion in 1991 but declared bankruptcy in 2001.

You will have seen the warning published by all investment houses that past performance is no guarantee of future returns. Be warned!

When a company and its shares become fashionable, so to speak, the price is driven up to levels at which the company no longer represents good value and so is not an attractive investment.

By way of example, the S&P500 is an index made up of 500 companies, but at the beginning of 2020 found itself dominated by five very fashionable companies. These companies were Microsoft, Apple, Google, Amazon and Facebook.

These are great companies, no doubt, but good value at any price? I think not.

Let us consider the the contribution of these five companies to the performance of the S&P500 index. In the decade to 10th February 2020 the sales of these five companies had grown from 1.9% to 7.9% of the total sales generated by all 500 companies in the index. At the same time profits from this group of five grew from 6.5% to 14.1% of the total profit generated by all 500 companies in the index.

Based on this information, how would you price these five companies relative to the total value of all 500 companies in the index?

Are they worth 7.9% of the index value based on their top line revenue contribution, or perhaps 14.1% of the index value based on their earnings contribution? Surely not more than 14.1%?

Would it surprise you to learn that they are priced at 20% of the entire value of the index? Five companies out of five hundred, that is 1% of the constituents of the index are priced at 20% of the value of the index.

Can that be justified or has their price run ahead of their intrinsic value?

Based on a back of the envelope estimate this suggests that they are over-priced by 41.8% [Calculated as: $(20.0\% - 14.1\%) / 14.1\% = 41.8\%$]

Even if the price is justified on the basis of expected future growth, then a 41.8% price premium means that their future success is already priced in. Said differently, if they perform in line with very high expectations then their intrinsic value will catch up with their price (which means little or no further upside for anyone investing today). Conversely, if these companies underperform expectations then they have a long way to fall back to reality.

On a risk versus reward basis, this does not look remotely attractive for a value investor.

The price has simply run ahead of of the underlying value of these companies. These companies are over priced, driven to over-inflated prices by speculative momentum driven investors.

So be warned that even the best companies can be poor investments at the wrong price (more on price later).

Investment risk is less a function of the individual company than it is of the price of that company's stock relative to its intrinsic value. This is not recognized by many investors.

Why would anyone buy these shares at over-inflated prices?

The answer is simple:

> 1. Many People tend not to understand the fundamentals of value investing but instead put their money in the most well known companies of the day.

> 2. Passive funds (which have become increasingly popular in recent years) invest blindly with little or no regard to underlying value.

Passive fund managers simply track a group of companies which may be defined by reference to an index, an industry, a geographic region or perhaps a combination of these factors.

If the mandate of the passive pension fund manager is to invest in large US tech companies, for example, then as people pay regular contributions into their pension the fund manager is obliged to invest that money within the tight parameters of his mandate. So he blindly buys companies, including Microsoft, Apple, Google, Amazon and Facebook, regardless of the market price and with scant regard to the underlying valuation of the company.

In this way passive investing, which may be renamed "blind faith investing", completely destroys the efficient pricing mechanism of the market. Instead the demand continues unabated pushing the market price ever higher.

To make matters worse, passive funds create concentration risk in the market. For example, in 2018 Microsoft, Apple, Google, Amazon and Facebook accounted for 13.3% of the S&P500 in terms of index weighting. The other 495 companies collectively account for 86.7% of the index. So consider what happens when Joe Public decides to move his portfolio of investments into a passive S&P500 fund. He is selling a diverse array of pre-existing holdings, many of which may be in small and medium sized enterprises, and now 13.3% of all his money will be invested in these five companies. Multiply that effect by the herd of investors who seem enamored by the fashion for passive funds and you have 13.3% of everyone's money being concentrated in these five companies! Small wonder their prices are over-inflated. There is an enormous amount of concentration risk in the market and the regulators really ought to take notice.

The corollary of this argument is that if too much money is being concentrated in a handful of companies at the expense of "non-fashionable" investments, then there is a great opportunity to be had from investing in those other undervalued assets which are being neglected (or overlooked) by the passive funds. Good investments are to be found far from the madding crowd!

Where shares in fashionable companies become over-priced the end result will be one of two things. Worst case scenario there will be a price correction (read "stock market crash") which will bring the price back down in line with the intrinsic value of the company. Best case scenario is that the share price growth will slow for many years (read "underperforming the market") until the value of the company catches up with the price. Either way,

I would not want to be holding these shares at the moment.

Microsoft is a perfect case study. In the year 2000 Microsoft was the darling of the stock market. It had a market capitalisation of $620 billion and it alone accounted for 5.3% of the S&P 500. It launched as a public company in 1986 and, in the 14 years that followed, it achieved staggering Compound Annual Growth Rates of 43% for sales, 51% for earnings and 68% for price. Note that price compounded far in excess of its top and bottom line expansion. The problems subsequently came not from the company but from its price. It was trading at 80 times earnings. Its price had simply run too far ahead of its intrinsic value. And so between 2000 and 2015 the stock underperformed the growth of the business, working off its over valuation. By 2019 revenues were still compounding at a healthy 9.4% per year and profits at 7.9%, yet the price only grew at 3.6% per year! The total return was 5.9% per annum if dividends paid are added to price growth, but still well below the hurdle rate to qualify as a value investment. Microsoft was a case of a great business at the wrong price – so let this be a warning to all of those investing in today's over priced stock market darlings!

So why not engage in shorting patently over-priced assets? The answer to this question was provided by the economist John Maynard Keynes:

> *"Markets can remain irrational longer than you can remain solvent!" John Maynard Keynes*

When buying a share with a high historic PE multiple many investors will justify an investment on grounds of rapid earnings growth resulting in the forward PE multiple being far more reasonable.

However, this is a dangerous strategy. Forecasting future earnings is almost impossible and unless there is intrinsic value in the investment at the point of investing these people are building a house on sand. Such investments are not classified as the value investments that you ought to be seeking.

That having been said an over priced share may still continue to climb in the short term and speculative investors may still make money on them. After all, it matters not if you over pay for an asset if there is a greater fool than you willing to pay a higher price.

There are, after all, a great many fools out there. Ensure that you are not one of them!

Accordingly, I have demonstrated that markets are inefficient in the short term but are exceptionally efficient over the long term.

The problems come when the fools stop buying, the market discovers that the house was built on sand and the whole thing comes tumbling down (read "asset bubbles bursting").

> *"...[Investment] history teaches us more about the nature of human beings than the nature of common stocks."*
> *Benjamin Graham*

And this leads nicely to the next chapter...

WE'RE FOREVER
BLOWING BUBBLES

Chapter Nine

T here are many fascinating historic examples of asset price bubbles.

Ranking as one of the most well known has to be that of the Dutch tulip market in the 17th century.

Tulips were originally introduced from Turkey in to Western Europe in the mid 15th century. They were admired for their extraordinary beauty and soon became a status symbol for the wealthy.

Tulips were cultivated into new and ever more exotic colour combinations and prizes were offered regularly for the grower of the best tulip.

In 1634 the tulip markets of the Netherlands, previously only available for professional growers, were opened to the public for the first time.

The increase in demand against relatively inelastic supply resulted in prices being pushed higher.

Dutch speculators learned about rising tulip prices and believed that they had found a risk free means of making money. They were willing to believe that prices would go on rising indefinitely.

The market price seemed not to matter because buyers were convinced that whatever the price today, it would be higher tomorrow ensuring a handsome profit.

As such, at the height of the boom people were paying more than one month's salary for a single tulip bulb. Each wave of new speculators fuelled the gains of the wave that came before them which only served to reinforce the myth of ever higher prices. A modern day Ponzi scheme operates on a similar basis.

To make matters worse, for the first time it became possible to buy tulip bulbs on a futures basis and also on attractive credit terms.

So buyers could buy on a leveraged basis without necessarily having the funds to pay. Instead they would seek to secure a bulb today with a view to selling it at a profit in the not too distant future before full payment was due.

By early 1637 many of the original participants in the tulip market, the professional growers, had taken their profits and retired on their windfall not believing their luck.

Suddenly on 3rd February of that year the stream of buyers dried up, probably due to the price having breached the affordability threshold for the common man, and the bubble finally burst.

Many people had their life's savings wiped out overnight.

The Dutch tulip bubble resonates with the buy-to-let property boom witnessed in the United Kingdom in the first two decades of the 21ˢᵗ Century. Perhaps people in the future will be writing about that asset bubble bursting in a similar fashion.

Not long after the tulip crash in the Netherlands, another bubble appeared in Europe. This centred on the floatation of the Darien Company in 1695.

The company was concerned with the establishment of a Scottish colony on the Isthmus islands of Panama.

The speculative frenzy was such that approximately one quarter of all Scottish currency in circulation was invested in the company.

The rapidly rising stock price attracted interest from far and wide as everyone seemed to want a piece of the action.

Shares were subsequently offered for sale in London, Amsterdam and Hamburg making it the first recorded international share offering.

It all ended disastrously when the Panama settlement failed and the company's shareholders lost everything.

There was no underlying value in the Darien Company. It was not producing profits and there was no coherent plan for how it might generate a sustainable return for investors. It was simply a speculative story in which people invested with blind faith.

An observer of the time wrote that "*things have no value in themselves, it is the opinion and fashion which gives them a value.*"

Indeed, despite notable advances in the quantification of risk in the late 17ᵗʰ Century [*remember back to our friends the Chevalier de Mere and Blaise Pascal*] Daniel Defoe, famously the author of Robinson Crusoe, but also a trader and a journalist of the time, commented that the speculation was driven by emotion and a gambling mentality which drove prices up well beyond their *intrinsick* [sic] value .

Irrational exuberance amongst the general public with a desire to get-rich-quick is at the very heart of every asset price bubble.

Lessons are never learned and history has a nasty habit of repeating itself.

The stock market crash of 1846 was brought about by a bubble in railway companies which then were a relatively new and revolutionary technology.

The steam engine first appeared in 1820; Queen Victoria made her maiden trip in 1842; and, suddenly everyone wanted to invest in railway companies.

By 1845 the entire country was consumed by railway mania and infrastructure plans had been submitted for the construction of over 8,000 miles of new track.

People had speculated well beyond their means. The infrastructure costs had been understated, calls for new capital were continually being made and each wave of investors saw its shares diluted by subsequent waves. This is not too dissimilar to the electric car company Tesla today.

It quickly became apparent that the investments were worth only a fraction of the price that had been paid for them.

Shareholders immediately sought to liquidate stock and the price collapsed. By summer 1846 bankruptcies were at an all time high, suicide was rife and many families were financially ruined.

Fast forward to modern times and the same cycle is readily apparent.

In the 1980s we witnessed the Japanese asset price bubble. Japan lowered its interest rates, bank lending was reckless and cheap money resulted in a misallocation of resources and subsequent asset price bubbles.

To make matters worse Japanese land and property prices had increased 5000% in the thirty years to 1986 and banks offered cheap debt against the security of land and property on the assumption that this growth rate would continue forever. So as property prices had run ahead of themselves so too had debt which was directly correlated in value to the land and property against which it was collateralised.

Cheap money was used to speculate on the stock market and valuations were pushed to eye-watering levels.

In 1987 the average PE multiple of a Japanese public company was 90. Fishery and forestry stocks were trading at 319 times earnings. Nippon Telegraph & Telephone reached 1,200 times earnings.

By 1989 the Nikkei index peaked at almost 40,000 which was up 27% on the year and 500% on the decade. Despite predictions that the index would double again over the next five years, instead the bubble burst.

By August 1992 the Nikkei index was 14,309 having lost 65% of its value. Tokyo property prices similarly dropped 60%. The net result was that Japan had dug itself into a recessionary hole where there was too much productive capacity (as the result of excessive capital expenditure prior to the crash) against a backdrop of too little consumer demand.

The recession that followed is still being felt 30 years later as the country found itself chained to low interest rates yet unable to sufficiently bring the economy back into balance. Decades of stagnation ensued.

The Japanese bubble is not too dissimilar to the situation in which Western economies now find themselves following the 2008 financial crisis. Interest rates were slashed to historic lows where they have remained for over a decade. Quantitative easing increased the supply of cheap money and asset bubbles have ensued in real estate, share prices and even in fixed-income products many of which have been pushed into negative yield territory.

For example, would it surprise you to learn that Microsoft, Apple, Google, Amazon and Facebook - five companies in the S&P500 index - had a joint market capitalisation (price) at the start of 2020 which was equal to the market capitalisation of all 500 companies in that same index at its 2009 low?

In fact, the S&P500 at 3,333 on 10th February 2020 has grown over 500% in a decade from its 2009 low when it stood at 666.

This means that the value of the the 500 companies in the index has compounded annually at 17.5% over the decade while GDP growth over the same period grew at approximately 2.5% per year.

Since GDP measures output of the economy, is it reasonable that the growth of the price of companies in the index should outpace the economy by so much over such an extended period? Think about this for a second and ask yourself this: does the valuation of the S&P500 at the beginning of 2020 represent economic reality or speculative euphoria?

I would suggest that it is a question of price running ahead of intrinsic valuation once again.

PART THREE

Learning to swim

YOU GET WHAT YOU PAY FOR, EXCEPT AT THE STOCK-EXCHANGE

Chapter Ten

To a salesman something is worth what someone else is prepared to pay. But to an investor price is somebody else's subjective assessment, while value is an intrinsic thing that may be measured objectively.

When investing you need to look at the quality of a company, its assets and the cash flow that its business produces. You quantify those things and you come to something named the intrinsic value of the corporation. If you pay full intrinsic value, you'll probably get a fair return; if you pay a premium to intrinsic value then you'll probably have an unsuccessful experience; but if you can buy for less than the intrinsic value then you should have an above-average return. That's value investing, and it is the intellectually soundest form of investing.

> *"Price is what you pay, value is what you get"* Warren Buffett

Subjectivity is influenced by sentiment and so price can fluctuate wildly around value.

For example, at year end 2015 the market capitalisation [read market price] of Berkshire Hathaway had fallen from $371 billion to $325 billion, meanwhile its normalised profits increased from $23 billion to $25 billion!

> *"Price fluctuates more than the value of a company and therein lies the opportunity for a good investor." Joel Greenblat*

Ultimately as an investor you ought to be looking out for opportunities where assets may be acquired at a discount to intrinsic value.

> *"The price is an integral part of every complete judgment relating to securities. In the field of common stocks, the danger of paying the wrong price is almost as great as that of buying the wrong issue." Benjamin Graham*

In terms of the deployment of investment capital, the returns will always be far greater when applied to an undervalued businesses. So while most stock market participants celebrate bull markets for rapidly rising stock and asset prices, the value investor will relish the opportunities that present themselves in a bear market.

If you were to invest in a private business you would be interested in the earnings power of that business. Said differently, you are concerned with the money that the business is generating day-to-day, year-to-year. This is your ongoing return on investment. You would not concern yourself on a daily basis with the price at which you may or may not be able to sell the business as a going concern.

This is the same mindset that you ought to adopt when investing in shares. Too many amateurs track market prices up and down, day to day, in the hope of achieving a short term capital gain. This is pure folly.

The truth is that most of the time the market is over exuberant and market prices do run ahead of value. This makes the deployment of investment capital difficult.

Empirical evidence shows that stock prices and earnings are mean reverting, so although they run out of kilter, over time they move together.

In 2018 for example, the S&P500 had a bad year dropping 4.4% despite earnings jumping 26.5%. The following year saw profits decline yet the index ended 2019 at a new high up 31.5%. Of particular note is that on average over this period the index had advanced 12.1% while operating earnings per share averaged 12.7% in the same period.

The lesson to be learned here is not to set unrealistic expectations for the growth of the shares in your portfolio. Over an extended period your benchmark ought to be the rate of growth of the earnings of your holdings. This is why, in the introduction to this book, I warned against the get rich quick speculative mind set. It also highlights the importance of selecting investments which show consistent strong earnings growth with good prospects to continue that success into the future.

Value generally progresses incrementally, often in correlation with changes in the growth and durability of the earning power of the business.

In exceptional circumstances value may suddenly undergo a

significant shift one way or the other. This could be a decline due perhaps to disruption, obsolescence or poor management; but it could also be an advance thanks to new discoveries or through shrewd strategic capital allocation.

A dominant competitive position in industry is important to durability of earnings over the longer term. If a firm is not the number one or number two player in its industry it may struggle to maintain its initial success and so by extension, its earnings power.

If a good share is held in a portfolio, growing its intrinsic value at an attractive annual rate, then you ought to be happy holding it for the long term, even forever.

If the price suddenly leaps well ahead of intrinsic value then this creates a dilemma for the value investor. Does he sell and then run the risk of sitting on cash (which is dilutive to the returns of his portfolio) while he seeks out a satisfactory alternative investment opportunity? Or does he continue to hold an over-priced asset?

It would, in truth, be preferable if the market did not get ahead of itself thereby avoiding this predicament. Similarly when new capital became available to invest from time-to-time it would mean that deployment would be easy, simply adding to existing holdings. Alas, we do not live in such a utopian world!

We have already discovered that prices have a habit of running ahead of value.

In 2019 the S&P 500 index generated a total return of 31.5%. The underlying businesses simply do not grow that fast and they do not earn that much on capital deployed. In fact, the combined businesses that make up the index saw their revenues and profits climb by approximately 4% over the same period!

At the beginning of 2020 the market was so over-priced that Warren Buffet's Berkshire Hathaway was sitting on $120 billion in cash because it was unable to find suitable value investments for the deployment of that capital. In fact, the situation became so acute that the company took the unprecedented step of seeking shareholder approval to utilise that capital in order to buy back its own shares!

The lesson to be learned here is that patience is virtuous as a value investor. If price dips below intrinsic value, grab the opportunity to invest. However, if price runs ahead of value you are best advised to sit on your hands and await a viable investment opportunity.

Never invest in haste!

BOOM AND BUST, RIDE IT BABY!

Chapter Eleven

A t the time of writing at the beginning of 2020, after the longest bull run in market history, investors are sanguine and happy to believe that the good times will roll-on forever, hence the buying continuing regardless of price.

At the other end of the spectrum, back in 2009 following the financial crisis and the collapse of Lehman Brothers Bank, investors were fearful and afraid to buy at any price.

Rather ironically amateur investors often have no idea of the true value of their investments because they are led purely by market sentiment rather than value. Their only measure of value is therefore the stock price, so in times of crisis, the more the price drops, the more they are inclined to sell.

This is the absolute opposite of the way in which a good investor ought to operate. A value investor should avoid the market when prices exceed his appraisal of fair value and he should be exploiting the buying opportunity when the market prices fall below fair value.

> *"Be fearful when others are greedy and greedy when the others are fearful"* Warren Buffett

Let us consider further these wise words of Mr Buffett.

During booms in the economy it is not uncommon for industries to become overcrowded and the markets that they serve to be over supplied. In times of crisis weaker companies will go insolvent and this is the way in which the market purges itself of inefficiency. It is nothing less than a survival of the fittest mechanism by which the survivors, the best run and strongest businesses, emerge with a greater market share of a resurgent market leading to fatter profits.

So buying wisely in a downturn is the course of action being advocated.

Value investing is not designed to outperform in a bull market. In a bull market (when prices are trending higher), anyone, with any investment strategy or none at all, can do well. It is only in a bear market (when prices are trending lower) that the value investing discipline becomes especially important because value investing, virtually alone amongst strategies, gives you exposure to the upside with limited downside risk.

In a market downturn, a momentum investor cannot find momentum; a growth investor will worry about an economic slowdown; and, a technical analyst will not like the look of his charts. But the value investing discipline tells you exactly what to analyse, price versus value; and then what to do, buy at a considerable discount and sell later near full value.

Because you cannot tell what the market is going to do, a value investment discipline is important because it is the only approach that produces consistently good investment results over a complete market cycle.

A recurring theme in this book is the fact that investing in a company, or in a share of a company, is a long term enterprise. If you cannot commit money to an investment with a long term time horizon, perhaps because you might need that money in the short term, then you should not invest at all.

Markets go through cycles. Some are severe and may be termed boom and bust, others are more mild perhaps seen in businesses with seasonal cyclicality such as tourism.

These temporary events have no bearing on the fundamental value of a business yet they have an enormous impact on price.

The price in the market is nothing more than a gauge of supply and demand at any given time. It is rarely a reflection of the true value of the asset.

Consider a turkey farmer taking his live stock to market. In the approach to Christmas, where turkey is the traditional meat of choice for the festive period in the UK, the turkey farmer will almost certainly find favourable prices for his produce. However, if the same farmer were to take those same turkeys to market a month later in January then he would almost certainly achieve a far lower price as demand has dissipated.

Has the intrinsic value of the turkey changed? No.

Should the farmer dump all of his turkeys in January because the price has collapsed? No.

All else being equal, the rational farmer will simply hold on to his stock until he is able to achieve what he considers to be a fair price.

So why do amateur stock-market investors behave differently? I have no idea the answer to this question, but I can assure you that they do.

Typically people own shares, demand drops from time to time depressing the price, and investors panic sell their investments.

It is rather like the children's story of *Chicken Little* who thought that the sky was falling down, went into a state of frenzied panic and acted in anticipation of that outcome. It is easy to let your imagination run wild when things do not go as planned, however the moral of the story is to have courage in the face of adversity.

> "...long-term shareholders benefit from a sinking stock market much as a regular purchaser of food benefits from declining food prices. So when the market plummets - as it will from time to time - neither panic nor mourn. It's good news..." Warren Buffett

The irrationality of other stock-market players is an opportunity for a savvy investor. A depression in the market price ought to be seen as an investment opportunity rather than an exit signal.

Warren Buffett once said that one of the three most important lessons that he learned from Benjamin Graham was that market price fluctuations are a friend of a value investor. They are to be welcomed rather than something to be concerned about.

> "Price fluctuations have only one significant meaning for the true investor. They provide him with an opportunity to buy wisely when prices fall sharply and to sell wisely when they advance a great deal." Benjamin Graham

However, a cheap price means nothing without an assessment

of quality. A poor company at a low price (perhaps on a multiple of earnings basis) is no less a poor company.

The objective, therefore, is to find a good company at a fair valuation which will allocate capital wisely and will grow to show you a good return on investment.

> *"The investment game always involves considering both quality and price, and the trick is to get more quality than you pay for in price. It's just that simple." Charlie Munger*

Value is determined by the operating results of the company - not by the price quotations in the market. The market may ignore business success for a while, but eventually will confirm it. Said differently, price fluctuations do not affect business values, although business values will eventually affect price. So, value relative to price, not price alone, must determine your investment decisions.

To the extent that price deviates markedly from value, opportunity presents itself, whether as a buyer or as a seller. Understanding the difference between price and value is perhaps the most critical aspect of investing.

Benjamin Graham liked to describe the investment process with reference to the parable of Mr Market which I shall reproduce here verbatim.

> *"Imagine that in some private business you own a small share that cost you $1,000. One of your partners, named Mr. Market, is very obliging indeed. Every day he tells you what he thinks your interest is worth and furthermore offers either to buy you out or to sell you an add-*

itional interest on that basis. Sometimes his idea of value appears plausible and justified by business developments and prospects as you know them. Often, on the other hand, Mr. Market lets his enthusiasm or his fears run away with him, and the value he proposes seems to you a little short of silly.

"If you are a prudent investor or a sensible businessman, will you let Mr. Market's daily communication determine your view of the value of a $1,000 interest in the enterprise? Only in case you agree with him, or in case you want to trade with him. You may be happy to sell out to him when he quotes you a ridiculously high price, and equally happy to buy from him when his price is low. But the rest of the time you will be wiser to form your own ideas of the value of your holdings, based on full reports from the company about its operations and financial position.

"The true investor is in that very position when he owns a listed common stock. He can take advantage of the daily market price or leave it alone, as dictated by his own judgement and inclination....Basically, price fluctuations have only one significant meaning for the true investor. They provide him with an opportunity to buy wisely when prices fall sharply and to sell wisely when they advance a great deal. At other times he will do better if he forgets about the stock market and pays attention to his dividend returns and to the operating results of his companies." Benjamin Graham

This is what is known as value investing and is an attempt to profit from the difference between calculated intrinsic value and market price.

If the market was made up of only active investors (those seeking value) then value trading would bring market price quickly into line with intrinsic value and we would have an efficient pricing mechanism.

However, passive investors and uninformed crowd-followers upset the market equilibrium and so there is often a dislocation between price and fair valuation.

This is no bad thing for the canny investor and the greatest amongst us agrees:

> *"An investor loves volatility and the idea of wild swings because it means more shares are going to be mispriced."*
> *Warren Buffet*

Too many amateur investors compare the current price to some former price which is silly.

Just because a share is trading 10% lower than it did last week does not mean that it represents value: perhaps it was 20% over priced last week and is now still over priced albeit less so!

Investors must never mistake an investment that is down in price for one that is bargain priced. Many shares that fall in price do so due to poor economic performance in which case the price falls in correlation to the value of the share.

This is very different to a share in which the price moves independently of value and so an investment presents itself at a price that is indeed at a significant discount to the true value.

> *"It is our argument that a sufficiently low price can turn a security of a mediocre quality into a sound investment opportunity." Ben Graham*

Although investments in mediocre companies that trade at bargain prices may be attractive as short-term investments, they are the wrong foundation on which to build a large and enduring portfolio.

The issue is one of return on both time and capital invested Buffett points out that with a mediocre company the gain sought is primarily in the closing of the gap between intrinsic value and market price. If this were to close relatively quickly after you invest then you will make a healthy return. But if it takes years for a revaluation then your average annual return on investments will be diluted substantially.

Being a mediocre company you would not want to hold it for too long as there is an opportunity cost in terms of the allocation of your capital in a better quality investment.

> *"Time is the friend of the wonderful business, the enemy of the mediocre... it is far better to buy a wonderful company at a fair price than a fair company at a wonderful price." Warren Buffett*

It is also psychologically difficult when you looked at a share when it traded at a lower price to now bring yourself to paying a higher price for it today. It is very common for an investor to say to himself that if the price gets back to a former level I will buy it, but that is a terrible way to think. This will result in many missed good opportunities

Warren Buffett always likes to look at investments without knowing the price because, he argues, if you see the price then it automatically has some influence over you.

No matter how accustomed we may have become to that former price of a security do not be distracted by it. The investment decision should be made solely on whether the company's fundamentals are significantly more or less favourable than the current financial-community appraisal of that stock.

You will find that the stock market is filled with individuals who know the price of everything, but the value of nothing. To that extent it is important to be stock-market agnostic.

Use price fluctuations to your advantage because they open up the opportunity to buy wisely when prices fall behind intrinsic value and to sell wisely when they run ahead of fair value.

When the price is between these two triggers the correct approach is to forget about the market and to simply collect your dividend returns, if any, and to allow the compounded growth of the business to take care of itself.

If you like the fundamentals of a particular businesses then appraise its value. If you are able to buy it at a favourable price relative to value then do so.

Look at the market merely as a place to go in order to buy and sell equities when you decide it is the right time to buy and sell; otherwise, ignore the stock market as it is an irrelevance, nothing more than a distraction.

In fact, many of the world's greatest investors, including Warren Buffett, Charlie Munger and Benjamin Graham have chosen to live and work as far away from Wall Street as they can because they wish not to be distracted by the white noise that emanates from financial centres.

The lesson to be learned is not to allow yourself to be pre-occupied by ever changing emotion or sentiment of the market. Similarly do not allow yourself to be drawn in to a *'too good to miss'* investment story that is circulating amongst the invest-ment community.

If the company is a good one then a little research will reveal that fact.

Ideally you want to find a hidden gem that others have yet to find: a company that is priced at a discount to its true value.

To find such a company takes work. There is no avoiding it.

As discussed in the opening chapters of this book, there is no magic formula. Indeed, we ought to be grateful that no such for-mula exists. If there were a quick and easy methodology that could reveal the true value of a company then everyone would use it, buyers and sellers alike, and price would never deviate from valuation meaning that good investment opportunities would entirely disappear.

You need to appraise a company for quality (qualitative ana-lysis) and also for its fundamental financial credentials (quanti-tative analysis) – more on both of these later.

The secret to good investing is to buy a share in a company on the same basis that you would buy the entire company.

Imagine that a friend of yours has a wonderful toy shop busi-ness that has good cash generative properties and which shows a nice return on invested capital. Your friend wishes to grow his business and asks you to invest in his company. How would you respond?

You would analyse the business performance historically and you would appraise its prospects for further growth. If you decide that this is a good investment opportunity you will acquire a share in the company and you will take a long term view.

You would not expect to double your money overnight but would anticipate steady growth over the years in which you are a co-owner of the business. So why would your expectations differ when buying a share in a publicly listed company?

The secret to good investing is to find excellent businesses that are favourably priced which you would be happy to own for an extended period (ten years is a good benchmark). If the business is a good cash-cow, milk it for as long as you possibly can.

> *"Regardless of price, we have no interest at all in selling any good businesses that Berkshire owns."* Warren Buffett

The economy will flow through cycles of boom and bust, but you would not panic and look to sell your stake in your friends company as soon as the stock-market dipped 10%. So why should you take a different approach when investing on the stock-market?

The mistake made by so many amateur investors is that they buy when the market price is inflated by optimism, and they sell when price is depressed by pessimism – said differently, they buy high and sell low.

In order to make money from the stock-market you will need to do the opposite - buy low and sell high.

Remember also that Investing is a zero-sum game. For every investor that out performs the market, there will be one or more offsetting investors that under-perform by a like amount. So the net return of all investors will, with one caveat, equal the return of the market as a whole.

The caveat is that the return of individual investors is subject to fees and costs, whereas the market index used as a benchmark is not. So the sum of all investor gains and losses will be the market return for the period less all transaction fees and costs.

Said differently, transaction fees and costs erode the returns of investors and so keep them to an absolute minimum by investing long term rather than buying and selling frequently.

This can only be achieved by carefully selecting companies in which you are happy to be an investor over the longer term. Again, ten years is a good time horizon.

Consider buying shares in the company as you would buying the company in its entirety. An investment in the shares of a business is an investment in an ongoing enterprise, it is not a lottery ticket. Think long term benefits not short term quick wins!

To cement this point, in 1996 Berkshire Hathaway issued its B-class shares in order to open up participation in the company to a wider array of investors. Warren Buffett issued an Owner's Manual for the benefit of its new shareholders in order to explain 13 owner related business principles. Principle 1 read as follows:

> "...I think of our shareholders as owner-partners...I hope that you do not think of yourself as merely owning a piece of paper whose price wiggles around daily and that is a candidate for sale when some economic or political event makes you nervous. We hope you instead visual-

*ize yourself as a part owner of a business that you ex-
pect to stay with indefinitely, much as you might if you
owned a farm or apartment house in partnership with
members of your family. For our part, we do not view
Berkshire shareholders as faceless members of an ever-
shifting crowd, but rather as co-venturers who have en-
trusted their funds to us for what may well turn out to be
the remainder of their lives...If we have good long-term
expectations, short-term price changes are meaningless
for us except to the extent they offer us an opportunity to
increase our ownership at an attractive price. " Warren
Buffett*

We shall explore the benefits of long term investing in more detail in the next chapter.

IT'S ALL ABOUT STAYING POWER

Chapter Twelve

T oo many people invest in the stock-market with a short term time horizon which is an act of sheer folly. They ask themselves for example, if tech stocks are due to bounce and then they buy in the hope that they can make a fast buck.

Many investors will look at short term macro-economic factors like GDP and try to read something into that.

However, with a long-term holding strategy the current state of the economy is of little consequence because the value of the company and so its shares will be determined by Owner Earnings over the long term.

Owner Earnings are a Buffett construct first mentioned in his 1986 letter to shareholders. We will explore this concept in detail later in the book.

There may be cyclical swings from time to time but a good company is a good company. An investment in a good company is a good investment.

Warren Buffett advocates keeping analysis as simple as possible. He has often joked about avoiding equations with Greek letters in them. These may be useful for a short term investor or when trading complex derivatives structures, but not for long term equity investments.

He has a fair point. You would not invest in an entire business on the basis of alpha, beta, delta or gamma, so why do it for a share of the business?

The correct mindset is to imagine that you are buying the company in its entirety rather than just a share in its equity. If the business is a good one and you would be happy to be an owner were it a private company, something that you would do with at least a five to ten year time horizon, then invest in a publicly listed company as a shareholder on the same basis. Why should it be different?

Warren Buffett once said that if you are not prepared to hold a share in a company for ten years then you should not be entertaining the prospect of holding it at all.

That is not to say that you will still be a shareholder in ten years time. Perhaps the price will race ahead of intrinsic value to the extent that you exit with a profit in six months or a year after investing, but you should not enter an investment in the expectation that this will be the case and evaluate the investment on a long term time horizon.

> *"Your goal as an investor should simply be to purchase, at a rational price, a part interest in an easily-understandable business whose earnings are virtually certain to be materially higher five, ten, and twenty years from now."*
> *Warren Buffett*

Benjamin Graham would often look for companies which were priced below the liquidation value of their assets. He noted that a revaluation of these companies will not occur overnight and typically takes four to five years. Once again this suggests investing in shares with a longer time horizon.

Yet another reason to invest over the long term is that the shareholders return tends from a modest Earnings Yields towards an often more attractive ROE.

The final argument for holding shares over the long term is that you avoid the dilutive effect of transaction fees. A trader that buys and sells frequently, even if he is successful in his stock selection, will give away a large proportion of his investment yield by paying transaction fees and taxes.

Since a good investor will look for the benefit of compounded returns over time a small difference on an annual basis can make an enormous difference to the compounded return over your investing career.

PART FOUR

Into the deep

TO PE OR NOT TO PE, THAT IS THE QUESTION

Chapter Thirteen

T he Price to Earnings (PE) Multiple is almost certainly the most commonly used measure of valuation by stock-market investors.

When used properly it may well be the best proxy for measuring value.

You need to ask yourself, "what price do I pay for a dollar of profit?"

Ultimately, that is what you are buying – a share in the profits of a company.

The answer will, of course, depend largely on how durable those profits are and the competitive position of the company. A company with a one-off opportunity to make money this year but not in subsequent years is worth far less than a business that churns out profit annually like a money making machine.

So the methodology to be adopted is relatively straight forward:

1. Determine what the real earnings of the business are cur-

rently (invariably not the number in the Income Statement or published in annual reports by the company);

2. Determine if earnings will grow, by what rate and for how long;

3. Determine the target holding period for the investment (5 years, 10 years, longer?);

4. Estimate the earnings of the company at the end of that holding period by compounding today's earnings at the growth rate;

5. Take into consideration the time value of money over that period by calculating the Net Present Value of those future earnings;

6. Multiply that annual number by a reasonable forward PE multiple for the company taking into account PE multiples of competitors and in the industry generally (historically PE multiples average 12 to 15 across the economy so a company trading at a PE multiple of 35 today is unlikely to be trading at that multiple in ten years from now).

So let us imagine that we are looking at a company with earnings of $8.49m and growing at a conservatively estimated 8% per annum. I invest with a 10 year time horizon and so calculate that the earnings in 10 years time, compounded at 8%, will be $18.33m. I conservatively assign a forward PE multiple of 10. The company has 116m shares outstanding and so the value of shares 10 years from now will be $1.58. I use a conservative discount rate of 10% and that suggests that the Net Present Value of that future share price is 61 cents. If I am able to buy the shares for less than this intrinsic valuation then, on the face of it, I have a good value investment.

Before investing you will still need to assess the quality of the company and that is a topic for a later chapter in this book.

When assessing earnings you ought to take an holistic view for the company having analysed historic data going back at least 5 years and preferably more. Do not use a snapshot in time which will invariably cause distortions that are misleading to the investor.

Too many investors lose sight of whether earnings are temporarily elevated or depressed. Consider for example the financial crisis of 2008 and 2009. At that point in time profits for many companies fell dramatically. As profits approach zero so the PE multiple ballooned. Did the high PE multiple mean that the company was a poor investment? No. And against normalised earnings (removing extraordinary data) that would have been evident.

Another example was the big changes to the corporate tax rate introduced by Donald Trump after being elected President. If the tax rate drops from 35% to 21% then corporate Net Earnings receive a 21.5% boost overnight [For every $100 of gross earnings you will now receive a net $79 rather than $65 due to the tax cut (a boost of 21.5%)].

You will, by now, be forming a picture in your mind that valuing companies for the purpose of investing is in fact more an art form than a mathematical science. As I said in the introduction, there is no magic formula. Ultimately judgement and experience play as much a part in success as does your aptitude for numbers.

It is also worthy of note that the PE multiple does not take account of net cash balances or debt. So two companies each with the same market capitalisation and generating the same earnings will have the same PE multiple, even if one company is debt free and the other is over leveraged.

The solution to this problem is to calculate the Enterprise Value (EV) to Earnings multiple which will be more revealing

CASTLES WITH A WIDE MOAT

Chapter Fourteen

I t is important not to confuse intrinsic value with book value. The latter, also known as shareholder equity, is simply the assets of the business less its liabilities.

It is perfectly normal for intrinsic value to diverge from book value as it is for price to diverge from intrinsic value.

> *"You can gain some insight into the differences between book value and intrinsic value by looking at one form of investment, a [university] education. Think of the education's cost as its "book value." If this cost is to be accurate, it should include the earnings that were foregone by the student because he chose college rather than a job.*

> *"For this exercise, we will ignore the important non-economic benefits of an education and focus strictly on its economic value. First, we must estimate the earnings that the graduate will receive over his lifetime and subtract from that figure an estimate of what he would have earned had he lacked his education. That gives us an excess earnings figure, which must then be discounted, at*

an appropriate interest rate, back to graduation day. The dollar result equals the intrinsic economic value of the education.

"Some graduates will find that the book value of their education exceeds its intrinsic value, which means that whoever paid for the education did not get his money's worth.

"In other cases, the intrinsic value of an education will far exceed its book value, a result that proves capital was wisely deployed.

"In all cases, what is clear is that book value is meaningless as an indicator of intrinsic value." Warren Buffett

Valuation metrics include Price-to-Book (PB) multiples, Price-to-Earnings (PE) multiples and Price-to-Sales (PS) multiples. In this chapter we will refer to these simply as the "Multiples".

These Multiples describe the premium, or discount, that the market is placing on the value of a company.

Many investors misunderstand the concept of value investing.

Low Multiples and a high dividend yield is often misconstrued by investors as indicative of a value investment.

Unfortunately, such characteristics, even if they appear in combination, are far from determinative as to whether a company is indeed a value investment.

The corollary of this is that a high Multiples and a low dividend yield are in no way inconsistent with a value investment.

Consider Microsoft for example. This company has what Benjamin Graham often referred to as a wide moat.

What did he mean by this?

Well if you were to have a castle with a moat around its perimeter then you make it very difficult for the enemy (a competitor in an economic context) to invade your stronghold.

In the same way, a company with an "economic moat" or competitive advantage has a dominant position in the market and formidable barriers exist to keep competitors at bay. This is why Microsoft remained a power house in the PC software space for over 30 years.

If you were to consider buying Microsoft shares as an investment back in March 2006 you would have been looking at a price per share of $20.26. This price implied a PB multiple of 4.93 and a PE multiple of 19.

The PB multiple is the premium which you are paying for the equity of the company. So for a price of $20.26 you would in fact be buying only $4.11 worth of equity in the company. That is quite a premium and many investors would baulk at paying almost five times equity.

Similarly the PE multiple implied a rather unattractive earnings yield of little more than 5%.

However, Microsoft is well run and has grown from strength to strength. If you had invested and were still holding your share in the company in December 2019 (13 years later) you would have found that not only had your $4.11 of equity compounded to be worth $14.47 (a CAGR of 10.17%), but that the PB multiple had actually expanded to 10.9, meaning that the market is now valuing the stock at almost eleven times the value of equity resulting in your $20.26 investment now being worth $157.70 (a CAGR or 17.1%).

The PE multiple expansion over the same period was from 19 to 27.50.

So buying an investment with high Multiples can be a good value investment. The question, therefore, is whether the company deserves the premium that you are being asked to pay and whether it is likely to defend that premium.
Microsoft had a very wide moat around its business – other companies found it very difficult to compete.

In fact, you may be interested to learn that the regulator considered Microsoft to be a de-facto monopoly towards the end of the 1990s because it had no viable competitors. This was a nice commercial position for the company, but a regulatory headache because the threat of being broken up loomed large.

The solution was that Bill Gates, CEO of Microsoft at the time, invested $150m into a weak competitor that was on its knees in order to keep it afloat so that there would be some kind of competition in the market for Microsoft.

That weak competitor was a company that you may have heard about – Apple.

Without the $150m cash injection Apple almost certainly would not exist today!

By 2003 Microsoft had sold its entire stake in Apple, but had it held on as a long term investor the $150m investment would have been worth $84 billion by the beginning of 2020!

So the lesson here is that an investor needs to consider how much of a moat a company has in the industry in which it operates and how defensible is that moat.

A low price earnings multiple by itself guarantees nothing and in many cases may serve as a warning indicator of a degree of weakness in the company. Said differently, other investors may have shunned the stock for a good reason causing it to have a justifiable weak price.

Do not fall into what market practitioners refer to as a "value trap" by buying shares of a company which looks cheap based on multiples but which will always be cheap because it has poor prospects.

Be warned, if you see a share that previously traded at $100 decline 99% to $1, before buying what may appear to be a bargain ask yourself why it declined so much. If it goes to zero then you still lose 100% of your investment!

The converse is also true however. Imagine a good company, an oil giant falling in price as the result a collapse in oil prices due to a short term OPEC dispute. The oil company will still be a good company after the dispute is resolved and will likely bounce back. This is what investors refer to as a "special situation" investment.

The good news is that a special situation recovery will see the bounce back being significantly higher then the initial drop (for example a 50% drop requires a 100% bounce to take the share back to where it began, similarly a 33% drop requires a 50% bounce and so on).

In any event, back to value investments, which are the subject of this book, Your growth as an investor will come from both the compounded growth of the equity in the company plus any expansion in the Multiples. It is essential to ensure that you achieve this combination rather than only one of these attributes alone.

For example, if you invest in a company in which you do not anticipate good compounded growth and only seek expansion of the multiples then the time that it takes for that expansion to occur, which could be several years, may defeat the viability of your investment.

> *"Time is the friend of the wonderful business, the enemy of the mediocre." Warren Buffett*

I must also caution that any contraction in the Multiples will have the opposite affect: it will dilute any compounded growth achieved. So in the case of Microsoft, imagine that it had expanded its equity by the same amount (from $4.11 to $14.47) but that a competitor was offering a superior product that was gaining traction in the market. In this case the PB multiple may have shrunk from 4.93 to perhaps 2.00 and so rather than having an investment worth $157.70, it would now only be worth $28.94 (your CAGR would now be 2.8% rather than 17.1%) and the investment could only be deemed to have been a very bad one.

So you will need to look at historic premiums commanded by the company's shares and the premiums of its competitors and ask yourself if the current Multiples are fair and defendable over the long term.

Also consider whether, in respect of the company's existing market position, it will be maintained, enhanced or perhaps lost.

As such, value investing must not be considered using one valuation metric in isolation. Instead value is a more relative concept which ought to be based on the expected growth rate of the company and the moat that it has around its business.

Said differently, a share trading at 30 times earnings but growing consistently at 25% per year with a wide moat can be much better value than a share trading at 7 times earnings but only growing at 3% and with no moat.

Microsoft is a company producing a product, computer software, which not only became entrenched in the world as a global standard but was a product that could be scaled up at very little marginal cost. You see, once the software is produced and has been sold to a large number of people, how much additional cost is there in selling it to one more person? The answer is little or nothing. And so Microsoft could sell its products to hundreds of millions of people almost as easily as it was able to sell to it's first million customers. Sales therefore grow rapidly.

By contrast, a company like Tesla has a large incremental cost associated with each additional sale. Scaling up car production is logistically difficult and expensive.

Similarly, if you have a business offering a bespoke architectural service, each additional customer carries a significant cost of providing the service and so not only are the profit margins more difficult to improve but scaling the business is not easy and so is very slow.

WHERE TO PUT THE PEG

Chapter Fifteen

T he PEG ratio is calculated by dividing the company's PE multiple by its expected earnings growth over an investment period (most investors use a projected five-year growth rate for earnings).

> *"The PE ratio of any company that's fairly priced will equal its growth rate". Peter Lynch, legendary investment manager.*

Said differently, a fairly valued company will have its PEG equal to 1.

It would therefore follow that a stock with a PEG ratio below 1.0 is to be considered exceptional value based on the growth rate that it is expected to show.

The PEG ratio has its critics. Among them is another legendary investment manager, Anthony Bolton. He argues that there may be two companies - one having a PE multiple of 5 and a growth rate of 5% per annum; the other having a PE multiple of 35 and a growth rate of 35%. While both of these companies have a

PEG or 1, investing in the second company will require a great deal of faith on the part of the investor that the 35% growth rate is sustainable. If not then the PE multiple will decline with the growth rate and the investor will suffer a multiple contraction. By contrast , the first company has a far more sustainable growth rate of 5% and so represents a better quality investment which may subsequently benefit from multiple expansion.

The argument is beyond dispute and so the PEG ratio should be seen as no more than a supplemental tool that needs to be taken in context, never to be used in isolation but alongside other metrics and quantitative analysis.

SALES AS A MEASURE OF VALUE

Chapter Sixteen

Another common technique to value stocks is the price to sales (PS) multiple. This is derived simply by taking the company's market cap and dividing it by its top line revenue number. All things being equal a low PS is good news for investors while a high PS can be a warning sign.

There is no hard and fast rule for what number is good and which are bad.

It is useful for comparing other companies in the same industry. The PS multiple will show whether the firm's shares are valued at a discount against others in its sector.

If we assume that the business has a PS multiple of 0.8 while its peers average a 2.5 this is *prima facie* evidence that its shares have a great deal of potential to appreciate in value if the PS multiple is to become more closely matched with those of its peers.

Some investors view sales revenue as a more reliable indicator of a company's growth than earnings, but sales figures must be coupled with profit margins data.

It should be noted that dividing the Profit Margin by the PS multiple provides us with the Earnings Yield, and so by extension the PE multiple.

$$\frac{Net\ Profit\ Margin}{Price\ /\ Sales\ Multiple} = Earnings\ Yield$$

Said differently, if you can buy $1 of sales for $1 then your earnings yield will be the profit margin. If it costs $2 then the earnings yield is only half of the profit margin and so on and so forth.

Accordingly, a strong company that enjoys fatter profit margins will typically have a higher price to sales multiple than a strong company with thin profit margins as earnings yields will invariably be similar.

Also the lower the profit margin the more sustainable it is likely to be. It certainly creates barriers to entry and so potentially provides the company with an economic moat.

Because this PS multiple is based on revenue rather than earnings it is useful for evaluating companies that are not yet profitable. That having been said, a value investor will generally shy away from companies yet to make a profit. He prefers to see the business become profitable and evidencing both stability of earnings and a clear path for growth.

A hitherto profitable company that subsequently makes a loss may also stop paying dividends and so lose its dividend yield. In this case the PS multiple represents one of the last remaining measures for valuing the business.

Finally, PS multiples may be used where a company has inconsistent earnings growth, Amazon being a perfect example. The Amazon PE multiple is relatively volatile from one year to the next, but the PS multiple is far more stable, as are its profit margins.

As we will see in the chapter entitled "All that glitters is not gold", a decision in relation to whether to capitalise or to expense an investment will have a profound affect on most valuation metrics except for the PS multiple.

Using Amazon's market cap of $901 billion and the company's 2019 fiscal year revenue of $280.5 billion, Amazon's PS multiple is 3.21

Generally, the lower the PS multiple the better but it is a relative measure and so needs to be compared to PS multiples of competitors in the same industry. It is not possible to compare PS multiples across different industries because profit margins will vary enormously. Remember that profit margin divided by the PS multiple is the earnings yield.

If the profit margin is only 3% you would want the PS multiple to be 0.5 or less in order to imply an Earnings Yield of 6% or more if that is your investment hurdle rate.

Consider the US retail giant Wal-Mart. For decades it had been a market leader and had displaced countless competitors, capturing ever greater market share. In 1999 it had 3% profit margin, a PS multiple of 1.5 which implied a 2% earnings yield (trading at a whopping 50 times earnings). At that time a poor investment despite being a great company.

Fifteen years later, with the profit margin still at 3% but the stock traded on a PS multiple of 0.33 which implied an earnings yield of 9.1% (much more attractive on 11 times earnings). Of particular note is that the share price had stagnated for 15 years with zero capital appreciation! Again, the moral of the story is that no matter how good the business, at the wrong price it makes a bad investment!

One further word of warning. The PS multiple takes no account of debt on the companies balance sheet. Two companies may show as having the same PS multiple, but one may be debt free while the other is over leveraged. The PS multiple will not assist in distinguishing one from the other.

This is a similar problem to that discussed when we looked at the PE multiple. The solution is therefore the same - use the Enterprise Value (EV)/Sales multiple.

Enterprise value is essentially the market capitalisation, plus long term debt less cash (so in effect you are adding net debt to the market capitalisation).

The EV/S multiple will distinguish between companies based on their debt profile. The more net debt that the company carries, the higher the EV/S multiple will be.

THE HIGHS AND LOWS
OF PROFIT MARGINS

Chapter Seventeen

Many amateur investors look for companies with fat profit margins. However, I would like to impress upon you that it is not the profit margin of a company that is important.

A company with a very thin profit margin can be enormously successful – Costco is a perfect example.

You may be interested to learn that most retail businesses do not break even until November each year (Black Friday, the first shopping day after the November Thanksgiving holiday in the US, is the day on which most retailers go from being in the red to being in the black – hence the name Black Friday). However, Costco is in the black at the beginning of each year before selling a single product. This is due to the revenue that it collects in membership fees. As such, it can afford to apply wafer thin margins to the goods that it sells, which in turn encourages more people to pay the membership fee in the following year. Perfect recurring revenue. A cash generating machine.

Profit margin is merely the profit made on each sale, so if sales volumes are high then the business can be enormously successful operating on small margins.

More particular, low profit margins often allow the business to both keep volumes high and to defend its business from competitors by creating a barrier to entry in to the market (a wide moat).

It would be difficult for a start-up to establish itself in a low profit margin environment because initially its sales volume will be too small.

Conversely, high profit margins make it easier for competitors to establish themselves which is not a situation that any company will want.

Consider McDonalds for example. This is a high volume low margin business which, let's face it, does not sell high quality gourmet cuisine. However, it is far more successful in terms of growth and earnings generation than any of the capital intensive Michelin starred fine dining restaurants owned and run by the world's best chefs, despite these businesses having much fatter profit margins on a far better quality product.

So if profit margin is not in itself the important factor for investors, what is?

You need to focus your mind on the changes in the amount of incremental capital required to produce an additional dollar of profit - the return on incremental capital is thus far more important. It is earnings as a percentage of invested capital, not sales, that really counts. Said differently, the return on capital (ROC)

Be aware that the sales generated on capital invested, otherwise known as capital turnover, multiplied by profit margin will give you ROC. So profit margin is an integral component of the relevant metric rather than being a relevant metric in its own right.

$$capital\ turnover \times profit\ margin = ROC$$

$$\frac{sales}{capital} \times \frac{earnings}{sales} = ROC$$

The absolute level of the profit margin is not particularly important without the context of capital turnover. The more capital required to produce one dollar of sales, the higher the profit margins need to be in order to generate the requisite ROC in order to incent marginal capital deployment. If the business is becoming more capital intensive, this represents an issue.

Changes in profit margins over time are important. Clearly an improvement in profit margins is what you are looking for. So you ought to compare profit margin data from one year to the next in order to ascertain whether a favourable trend exists.

In many instances a lower profit margin business may be preferable for the following reasons.

First, an increase in profit margin from 1.5% to 2% will have the same impact on returns as an increase from 12% to 16%, yet the former may well be easier to achieve.

Second, a business that is able to convert its capital investment into large volume sales can afford to operate on much thinner margins and so build a wide moat to protect its franchise. The McDonalds model versus the gourmet restaurant model being the perfect example.

In my experience, the lower profit margin businesses are amongst the most durable in terms of longevity, which is exactly what you want as a long term investor.

This leads nicely to the next chapter where we will consider the return on capital or ROC along with ROE.

JAMES EMANUEL

ROE, ROE, ROE THE BOAT
TO A BETTER YIELD

Chapter Eighteen

There are a multitude of valuation metrics but three will form the focus of this chapter. The PE multiple, the PB multiple and Return on Equity (ROE).

Using an analogy to introduce these valuation tools, imagine you invest in a buy-to-let house.

Now let us say that you bought the house for $1m in the knowledge that the house is generating a rental yield of $125,000 a year. Assuming that no debt was used to buy the house (it was a cash purchase) then your equity in the house is the full $1m and you are receiving a 12.5% ROE. The price at the point of purchase is eight times earnings ($1m/$125k) and so your PE multiple is 8.

Interest rates are cut, share prices soar as money floods into the stock-market chasing better returns which results in dividend yields falling in line with interest rates, and the rental yield sought on a property also drops pushing up property prices.

So now we assume that there are buyers of buy-to-let real estate with an investment hurdle rate of 6.25% rental yield. Against the $125,000 rental income produced by your house this implies an intrinsic value of $2m for the house.

You purchased the property at a price below intrinsic value (exactly what the value investor is looking for).

Your book value or equity (synonymous terms) remains $1m as this is the value for the asset on your balance sheet (the price that you paid).

The PE multiple has moved from 8 ($1m/$125k) to 16 ($2m/$125k). This implies that the Earnings Yield moved from 12.5% to 6.25%.

Since the book value is fixed and independent of price, the equity remains at $1m and so the ROE (Return on Equity) will continue to be 12.5%

The PB multiple was one (the price that you paid was equal to the book value of the asset) but now the market price is twice the book value and so the PB multiple is 2 ($2m/$1m). This means that anyone buying the property from you will achieve an Earnings Yield of 6.25%.

Hopefully you are now getting a picture of how these metrics assist with the valuation of assets.

You may or may not have noticed a relationship between the three valuation metrics discussed.

$$Earnings\ Yield = \frac{ROE}{PB}$$

and

$$Earnings\ Yield = \frac{1}{PE}$$

so

$$\frac{ROE}{PB} = \frac{1}{PE}$$

The one over PE relationship is logical. If I buy an asset for $10 and it gives me a $1 return then the price to earnings ratio is 10/1 = 10. The Earnings Yield is the reciprocal of the PE multiple, that is to say 1/10 = 10%.

Understanding this relationship is very important to assessing the valuation of any investment particularly when buying shares.

I have deliberately chosen to use real estate in my example to demonstrate one other very important issue for a value investor.

Assets which depreciate over their useful life, for example a piece of software or an item of machinery, will see their balance sheet value reduced every year and a corresponding charge added to the income statement. In this way the cost of the asset is spread over time for the purpose of calculating the profitability of the business.

The situation is not so straight forward when an asset appreciates in value, particularly where the value is assessed using market price. This methodology is commonly referred to as mark-to-market. As we know only too well, market prices oscillate up and down over time and this presents a problem for an accountant. Examples of assets which fluctuate in value may include marketable securities (such as shares in another company), a football player or, as in our example, real estate property.

The most common approach to dealing with this issue is to simply hold the asset on the books at the lower of cost price or depreciated value. So for an appreciating asset this will invariably mean cost price.

This is what I have demonstrated in my example. The book value of the property remains at $1m, notwithstanding its market price of $2m.

Why is this so important?

Well it has a bearing on the valuation and profitability metrics for the company.

Because the book value of this property remains unchanged at $1m, its ROE is unchanged at 12.5%. Anyone looking from the outside may be impressed by such a healthy return on equity – but should they be impressed?

The 12.5% ROE is an historic profitability number based on an historic valuation of the asset. It is no reflection of the ability of the management. Indeed, the management would not be able to scale its business by deploying new capital (perhaps reinvesting retained profit) at that same rate of return.

So it is fair to say that the ROE measurement is misleading for an investor. The investor is more concerned with the rate of return at which the management is able to deploy new capital to grow the business.

So let us consider once again the relationship between ROE, PB multiples and Earnings Yields.

$$Earnings\,Yield = \frac{ROE}{PB}$$

In the context of our example, the income generated remained unchanged at $125k. The book value or equity on the balance sheet is also unchanged at $1m, but the market price changed from $1m to $2m.

What does this mean for our valuation metrics?

As discussed, ROE remains at 12.5% because earnings and equity valuations are unchanged, but the PB multiple goes from 1 ($1m price / $1m book value) to 2 ($2m price / $1m book value).

The result is that the Earnings Yield moves from 12.5% to 6.25%.

Had the company decided to revalue its asset on its balance sheet (which it is perfectly at liberty to do) then the equity value would have changed from $1m to $2m, against our constant $125k earnings results in a 6.25% ROE. In this situation the PB multiple would have remained at 1 ($2m price / $2m book value) which, once again, results in an Earnings Yield of 6.25%.

The lesson to be learned here is that the Earnings Yield is a more reliable indicator of the return that an investor ought to expect than is ROE.

Also, we can observe that whether or not the appreciating asset is revalued by the company, the PB multiple is the metric that balances the equation.

ROE can often be misleading for a multitude of reasons. One, as we have learned here, is the carrying of assets at historic cost price rather than true value. Others include the write-off or writing-down of non-performing asset values and the repurchase of a company's own shares at a premium price, both of which erode shareholder equity (more on these later).

If the combination of ROE and PB multiple result in an Earnings Yield that meets your hurdle rate for investing, then the shares should remain on your eligible investment list. However, further analysis will be required before you are ready to pull the trigger!

The key lesson here is that a high PB may be justified where the book value of assets does not reflect economic reality. So in our example, a PB multiple of 2 does not mean that the asset is over priced (the numerator is not the issue) it simply means that equity is under valued on the balance sheet (the denominator is too low).

> *"Today, our emphasis has shifted in a major way to owning and operating large businesses. Many of these are worth far more than their cost-based carrying value. But that amount is never revalued upward no matter how much the value of these companies has increased. Consequently, the gap between Berkshire's intrinsic value and its book value has materially widened..." Warren Buffett.*

So a company which has a balance sheet of appreciating assets will naturally see its PB multiple expand over time.

However, a high PB multiple for a company without appreciating assets may suggest that either the market price is unrealistically high, the company is engaged in over priced share buybacks or the management has engaged in write-offs or write-downs of assets. All three of these warrant further analysis on the part of the investor.

While the PB multiple is useful when evaluating banks and other financial institutions that carry a large number of assets on their balance sheets, it far less useful for asset-light business models such as tech companies or those in the service sector.

When you buy shares in a company you will generate a return by way of three mechanisms:
1. intrinsic growth of the company and so its value;
2. dividend payments; and,
3. multiple expansions (or you will diminish your return by way of multiple contraction).

By way of simple example, assume that your investment has a PB multiple is 2 and a book value of $10m. The price of the company on the market will be $20m – simple maths.

If the company expands while you are a shareholder to have a book value of $15m then provided the PB multiple remains at 2 the value of the company will increase by 50% to $30m. Your shares will appreciate by the same amount as the company growth rate.

But imagine that the PB multiple expands to 3. Now the company is worth $45m and so your investment has increased by 125%. This is multiple expansion.

If the PB multiple had contracted to 1 over the same period, then despite the book value having increased from $10m to $15m, the market price of the company will have contracted from $20m to $15m and so 50% corporate growth has been eroded and has become a 25% investment loss by way of multiple contraction.

"To the extent possible, we would like each Berkshire shareholder to record a gain or loss in market value during his period of ownership that is proportional to the gain or loss in per-share intrinsic value recorded by the company during that holding period. For this to come

> *about, the relationship between the intrinsic value and the market price of a Berkshire share would need to remain constant, and by our preferences at 1-to-1. As that implies, we would rather see Berkshire's stock price at a fair level than a high level. Obviously, [we] can't control Berkshire's price. But by our policies and communications, we can encourage informed, rational behaviour by owners that, in turn, will tend to produce a stock price that is also rational." Warren Buffett.*

An investor ought to be wary of an overpriced investment with a high PB attached in circumstances where the PB is likely to decline and so erode the return on his investment by way of multiple contraction. But if the PB multiple is high and likely to remain high (as in the case of a company with appreciating assets), or better still where the multiple may expand further, then the investor will benefit from multiple expansion of his investment returns.

The key lesson here is not to shy away from a potential investment purely because it has a high PB multiple without first having gained an understanding of why it is high and where it is likely to be in future.

Incidentally, multiple expansions and contractions can be calculated using any price multiple (Price to Earnings , Price to Sales or Price to Book).

Now that you understand how price multiples work we need to explore further the relationship between Earnings Yield and ROE.

Let us assume that you invest in a company ABC Inc which has an ROE of 12.5%, a PB of 2 and so an Earnings Yield of 6.25%.

So, as an investor if you receive the Earnings Yield of 6.25% why should you care about the 12.5% ROE number?

At first glance you could be forgiven for thinking to yourself that the earnings yield number is all that matters.

If you were a short term investor then Earnings Yield is indeed the best that you may hope to achieve, but as a long term investor your return on investment will gravitate towards the Return on Equity gradually over time.

Allow me to explain why that is the case.

Imagine that you buy a share in ABC Inc for $2.

The PB multiple is 2, which means that you are paying twice as much for the equity that you acquire in the company than its book value. Said differently, you are in fact only buying $1 of equity for $2.

If the company is earning 12.5% on equity, then the return on the $1 of equity purchased will be 12.5 cents. Those earnings as a percentage of the $2 price that you paid is your earnings yield of 6.25%

Now imagine that the ABC Inc is growing and the management reinvest that 12.5 cents in the company rather than paying any of it out as a dividend. So the assets of the company grow by 12.5 cents and, all else being equal, your $1 equity stake grows to a $1.125 equity stake in year two of your investment.

The $1 that you initially purchased is still earning a 6.25% yield due to the premium that you paid for it, but the earnings reinvested by the company will be generating the full 12.5% ROE because no premium has been paid for that part of your equity holding.

Assuming that ROE remains at 12.5%, in year two the earnings of the company attributable to your equity stake will be 12.5

cents (as in year one) plus 1.6 cents on the element by which your equity stake has grown. So in total you earn 14.1 cents in year two. As a percentage of the $2 that you paid, 14.1 cents is 7.05% (better than the 6.25% earned in year one!).

And this is again reinvested by the management in the company so your equity stake grows to $1.226. And in year three you earn 12.5 cents + 2.825 cents, or 15.325 cents in total. Now your total return on your initial investment is 7.66%.

And so this process goes on.

By year six your equity stake will have more than doubled. So now less than half of your equity holding is earning 6.25% while the majority is earning 12.5%. Your average return is 9.375%.

So now you can see how the return earned on your investment has shifted from 6.25% in year one to 9.375% in year six. And every year it will tend closer and closer to the 12.5% ROE.

The one caveat to be aware of is that ROE is a levered metric. Earnings are generated on total capital which is a blend of equity and debt. Measuring those same earnings against equity alone means that the more debt employed in the business, the more exaggerated the ROE metric becomes. What the company is really generating is a return on capital (ROC) which may be considered to be the unlevered return on equity.

Of course if the company has no debt then ROE and ROC will be the same, but the more debt that the business has on the balance sheet, the bigger the differential between the two profitability ratios will be.

And so it follows that as the company retains earnings and enjoys compounded growth of its equity valuation, the thing that needs to be understood is what happens to the debt profile of the business.

If the company reduces debt as the value of its equity grows then what happens to ROE? If debt is replaced by equity then total capital remains unchanged and so ROE will tend lower towards ROC. However, if the company maintains its debt to equity ratio by increasing its debt as the value of its equity grows then the differential between these profitability ratios may remain unchanged (assuming that opportunity exists to reinvest capital at the same rates of return).

As companies grow in size, so their opportunity to continue growing at the same rate diminishes. When a new start up makes its second sale it has doubled its turnover in an instant - 100% growth. However, when it has made $100 million in sales it will not be as easy or as quick to get to $200 million. This is sometimes referred to as the 'law of diminishing returns."

> *"...we think very few large businesses have a chance of compounding intrinsic value at 15% per annum over an extended period of time..." Warren Buffet.*

And so when you are calculating how equity is likely to compound in value over time, factor the law of diminishing returns into your calculations.

A simple and relatively conservative way to do this might be to estimate the likely return on equity that the company will generate ten years from now, based perhaps on other more mature companies in the sector, and then assume that ROE will reduce on a straight line basis between the two points (a linear interpolation). This can be built into your pricing model.

Well I hope that you now fully understand the relevance of ROE, PE multiples, Earnings Yields and the PB multiples when considering an investment.

Throughout this book I have sought to point out arguments in favour of long term investing – a buy and hold strategy. The annual increase in returns on investment and the compounded growth of the intrinsic value of the company is perhaps one of the strongest reasons to adopt a buy and hold strategy.

If you were to buy and sell frequently then the best that you could hope for would be the earnings yield which is more often than not significantly inferior to the ROE.

HAVING A BREAK DOWN

Chapter Nineteen

Remember that return on equity is calculated by the earnings of the company divided by the equity of the company.

In the previous chapter we explored how a long term investment strategy allows the investor to improve on the annual returns on his investment by allowing Earnings Yield to gravitate towards ROE over time.

And so it follows that the greater the proportion of earnings that are retained to be re-deployed in the company, the faster the business ought to grow and so the stronger will be the gravitational pull towards ROE.

So pay particular attention to the Retained Earnings Ratio or the Payout Ratio (which is the percentage of earnings paid out as dividends – the remainder being retained).

Needless to say that this beneficial affect requires that the retained earnings be deployed at incremental returns at least as great as their current ROE.

As with all profitability ratios ROE should not be viewed as a snapshot of time. Instead look at the consistency of ROE over consecutive years and also the trend in order to give you an idea of how ROE might change during the term of your investment.

By analogy, if I were to tell you that a football team won today's game, would you know if they were a good football team? Or would you need to look at the track record of previous results in order to formulate a proper opinion?

The same is true for evaluating a company.

Ideally you ought to look at a broad picture of metrics over at least the past five years.

It is for this reason that so many financial data websites and numbers published in newspapers are absolutely useless. You will see a single snapshot metric for today and absolutely no context or perspective on trends or historic data.
So a word of caution, be choosy when it comes to the source of the data that you use for making investment decisions.

The best source of data is the company itself which means trawling through annual reports for the past few years, all of which may be found on the company's own website.

While the return on equity is a great indicator, beware that ROE may be enhanced in any number of ways, not all of them favourable to the investor. Further investigation is always required as I shall go on to explain.

Equity for many companies can be severely understated as discussed in the previous chapter. Assets are often carried at historic depreciated cost rather than at replacement cost thereby shrinking book value.

Write-offs and write-downs reduce assets on the balance sheet and so also the corresponding equity values.

Finally, share repurchases at increasing premiums to book value drive book value lower. (More on write-offs, write-downs and share buy-backs in the chapters devoted to those topics.)

In all of these cases an understated equity value would cause an increase in the ROE metric because the denominator in the calculation is reduced.

As such improvements in ROE will not necessarily be a reliable indicator of a good investment opportunity. However, if ROE is increasing for the right reasons then improvements in ROE are a very positive investment signal.

What we need is a greater understanding of what ROE actually means for an investor. So let's break it down into components.

The executive team at a chemicals company named DuPont dissected ROE in order to provide better insight for the purposes of managing their company.

That methodology is now known as DuPont analysis, and I'll explain how it works.

Remember:

$$\frac{Earnings}{Equity} = ROE$$

So if my earnings were $10m on $50m of equity I have a ROE of 20%.

Now consider this:

$$\frac{Earnings}{Sales} \times \frac{Sales}{Assets} \times \frac{Assets}{Equity} = \frac{Earnings}{Equity} = ROE$$

Now we have dissected ROE in a format which allows us to understand what is happening beneath the surface. Let's investigate each component in turn.

- Earnings over Sales is otherwise known as Net Profit Margin – If ROE is improving because Net Margins are increasing then that is clearly good news.
- Sales over Assets is otherwise known as Asset Turnover – this number provides evidence of how efficiently the company is utilising its assets in order to produce sales. If ROE is increasing because of Asset Turnover is improving then this is also good news.
- Assets over Equity is otherwise known as Leverage – an investor would prefer to see this metric decreasing in value because as equity makes up a larger proportion of assets it is clear that liabilities and in particular debt is decreasing. It therefore follows that if ROE improves because leverage is increasing then this is not a good thing.

As an example, consider the companies in the following table:

	Company A		Company B	
	Year 1	Year 2	Year 1	Year 2
Net Profit Margin	0.09	0.08	0.09	0.1
Asset Turnover	1.2	1.2	1.2	1.4
Leverage	1.85	2.6	1.85	1.64
ROE	20%	25%	20%	23%

If you were to look at ROE alone you would consider Company A to be a better investment because it has grown its return on equity far more than Company B.

However, applying the DuPont analysis you will form an entirely different opinion. We see that Company A has seen its profit margin shrink by 1% (bad news), it has not improved its efficiency and its leverage has increased considerably (very bad news, particularly since the additional debt has not resulted in any noticeable improvement to profitability or efficiency).

Company B on the other hand has reduced its leverage, increased its profit margin and improved its efficiency in terms of asset turnover.

Company B is the easy winner and, given the choice, would be my preferred investment.

The lesson to be learned here is never to judge a book by its cover. Always scratch beneath the surface.

A similar approach may be adopted for a range of financial metrics.

Consider once again the Earnings Yield. This may be dissected as follows:

$$\frac{Net\ Profit\ Margin}{Price/Sales\ Multiple} = Earnings\ Yield$$

So it follows that a company with a 20% net profit margin and a PS multiple of 5 will have an earnings yield of 4%. But a company with an 8% net profit margin and a PS multiple of 2 will also have an earnings yield of 4%.

With the same earnings yield, which company would you rather invest in?

It might be argued that the first company will struggle to maintain such a fat profit margin. Such a profitable business will attract fierce competition which, over time, will compete margins away. This would result in either a drop in Earnings Yield (with a corresponding increase in the PE ratio) or a drop in the PS multiple. Either way this will negatively impact the share price.

The second company may therefore be a better long term investment.

When looking at ROE, also consider Return on Capital (ROC) and Return on Assets (ROA).

When looking at ROC, remember that Capital = Debt + Equity. Asset values can be understated and so misleading but take comfort that it is very difficult to understate the other side of the balance sheet, particularly the debt element.

To the extent that companies fund operations and share-repurchases with debt, that portion of capital is properly identified, making the return on capital a critical acid test of profitability when companies employ increasingly large amounts of leverage.

By way of example, imagine that a company has no debt and $10m of Equity - the total capital is therefore $10m. If it deploys that capital to generate $1m of earnings then the ROE is 10% and the ROC is also 10%. Now imagine that in the following year the company takes on $2.5m of debt - the total capital increases to $12.5m. If the revenue increases pro-rata to the increase in capital then revenue will increase to $1.25m. Now the ROE has increased to 12.5% while the ROC remains at 10%.

Since you want to know how well management deploy capital, as the company deploys more debt the ROC number becomes more important.

For the same reason, because each company will use different debt ratios thereby flattering ROE to different extents, ROC is a far better indicator than ROE for the purpose of comparing one company to another within an industry sector. It will help you to understand how efficiently management deploys capital within the business.

Once you have short listed attractive companies for investment, ROE plays a part in allowing you to assess your likely returns as a shareholder and so may assist in making a final investment selection from your short list.

In relation to ROA, if the trend is upward then this indicates that the business is becoming more efficient because it is extracting more of a return out of its assets year on year. If the trend is downward then you ought to investigate why this is the case and understand whether this presents a material investment risk.

Any risk needs to be assessed for materiality and then a decision about whether to invest or not can be made.

Consider also that the company's assets are made up of both tangibles and intangibles.

Tangibles include cash and short term investment, inventory, receivables and PPE (Property, Plant and Equipment). These are the hard assets used to generate revenue.

Intangibles may include intellectual property such as brand names or patented processes. It will also include Goodwill which is the premium that is paid for another company during an acquisition. Said differently, it is the amount that a company pays for another company over and above the target company's book value.

Good investors are interested in the return that a company earns on net revenue generating assets, sometimes referred to as 'net tangible assets'.

Net Tangible Assets (NTA) is calculated as total assets less total liabilities less non-revenue generating intangible assets (such as goodwill). The par value of preferred stock should also be deducted if applicable.

This is essentially an alternative measure of equity – it is the same as Equity less non-revenue generating intangible assets. So return on NTA is an alternative measure of ROE.

Some intangible assets are revenue generating capitalised assets which will need to be either renewed or replaced over time, for example a patent on a new drug for a pharmaceutical company. These, therefore, ought to be included in the Return on Net Tangible Assets calculation.

In 1972 Warren Buffett invested in See's Candies Inc. At the time the company was earning $2 million in revenue on $8 million in net tangible assets. See's Candy was analysed alongside another company earning the same $2 million in revenue but on a base of $18 million in net tangible assets.

Both companies generate the same revenue and have similar earnings and cash flows so many investors would look at them as equivalent investments.

But in order to double sales See's Candy will require an additional $8 million in net tangible assets while the other company needs an extra $18 million. For the second company, since it has to invest more than twice as much money to grow by the same amount, not only will that be more difficult to achieve, but whether that additional capital is raised by way of debt or new equity, it will result in lower rates of return for existing shareholders.

This helps to illustrate why using only earnings per share and cash flow can lead the investor astray over time.

Additionally, growth rates alone can be misleading if the investors have no idea of how much capital will be consumed by the company along the way.

In fact, Warren Buffett warns that growth rates have nothing to do with valuation except to the extent that they provide clues to the amount and timing of cash flows into and from the business. Indeed, he warns, that growth can destroy value if it requires cash inputs in the early years of a project or enterprise that exceed the discounted value of the cash that those assets will generate in later years.

So the more money that a business is able to generate from its net tangible assets, the better. This is what the Return on Net Tangible Assets will tell you.

By contrast, conventional metrics such as ROA (all assets) are distorted by non-revenue generating assets on the balance sheet because the denominator is so much larger, thereby painting a less reliable picture for the investor.

PART FIVE

Beware of the sharks

SHARE REPURCHASES / STOCK BUY-BACKS

Chapter Twenty

S tock buy-backs have become commonplace in the market and while these are sometimes well intentioned and beneficial for the shareholder, too often they are not.

Share buy-backs are among the most misunderstood and also the most abused aspects of modern capitalism.

A repurchase operation will be presented as a means of returning value to the shareholders.

Unfortunately the truth is that buy-backs will likely destroy shareholder equity and are nothing more than a means of the management pursuing a self-serving agenda.

Performance based pay can make the management team and board members exceptionally rich. Too much of the wealth being created by many businesses is being transferred to Chief Executives and their minions rather than finding its way to the shareholders where it belongs.

So, motivation for management buying back the company's own shares may include a desire to manipulate key performance indicator (manipulate is a strong word and I use it deliberately). Not only does this assist the executives in painting a rosier picture of their own performance, which helps secure their tenure, but it also enhances their own personal remuneration. Much of the time it is nothing more than smoke and mirrors being used to deceive shareholders.

Consider the impact of a share repurchase operation:

- It will reduce the number of shares outstanding thereby increasing earnings per share (EPS) relative to prior years.
- The announcement of an intention to repurchase shares by a company sends a message to the market that the management deem the company's shares to be cheap, thereby stoking demand. In any event the buy-back itself adds to natural demand for the shares which, all else being equal, pushes the share prices higher.
- It will allow executives to deliver a constant dividend per share year on year with less cash if the number of shares outstanding is reduced.
- It will mask or offset the dilution to shareholders that comes from executive compensation paid in shares.
- When executed above book value (most of the time) it will enhance ROE by eroding equity despite earnings being unchanged or worse, declining.

This last bullet is critically important and not particularly well understood by either shareholders or by many finance directors. Accordingly I shall use this opportunity to explain how this works in practice

Share buy backs only really make commercial sense where the PB multiple is less than 1.00 because that is accretive to the equity value of the company and so beneficial to the shareholders. Conversely, paying more than book value erodes shareholder value.

By way of example, imagine owning a $1m house equally with your partner. You also have $750,000 cash in the bank, so the total value of your assets is half of the house $500,000 plus £750,000. A total of $1.25m. You offer to buy your partner's 50% share which has a book value of $500,000 (half of $1m).

You ought to be happy paying anything up to $500,000 (PB less than or equal to 1) but not paying more than that number. Buying at a premium (where the PB multiple is greater than 1) erodes the total value of your assets by the amount of the premium paid (see table below).

Your Assets prior to the deal	Price of partners $500k equity	PB multiiple	Your Assets after the deal	Net change to your total Assets
$500k equity in 50% of the house + $750k cash = **$1.25m**	$400k	400k/500k = 0.8	$1m equity in the house + $350,000 cash = **$1.35m**	+ $100k
	$500k	500k/500k = 1	$1m equity in the house + $250,000 cash = **$1.25m**	No change
	$600k	600k/500k = 1.2	$1m equity in the house + $150,000 cash = **$1.15m**	- $100k

The same situation is true for shareholders when using company money to buy-back shares at a premium to book value.

So when a company uses surplus cash on the balance sheet in order to buy-back shares when the PB is greater than 1 it is de-facto, eroding shareholder equity in the company.

The only caveat to this is where the PB multiple is high as a result of appreciating assets being carried at historic cost rather than at their true economic value. In such circumstances the PB multiple is not a reliable indicator because equity is severely understated.

So why would management choose to erode shareholder value?

Well, some managers are poor at capital allocation (the most important job for a corporate executive). They may be naive and not fully appreciate that their decision is in fact destroying shareholder value. In this case, run for the hills and do not invest in a company with incompetent management teams.

At the other end of the spectrum are managers that do understand the impact on shareholders of overvalued share repurchases but pursue this strategy regardless.

Remember that Equity = Assets minus Liabilities. So as the Asset value of the company is eroded by embarking on an overvalued share buy-back strategy, so too is the Equity value of the company.

If corporate earnings remain unchanged, then when calculating Return on Equity (ROE) the numerator (the profit/return) will be the same but the denominator (the Equity) will be smaller. The net result is that ROE numbers look to have improved.

Hey presto! Magic! The management pulled a rabbit out of the hat and the shareholders clap and cheer, not realising that it is just an illusion!

Not only has the ROE improved, so too has the ROA (return on assets) and the ROC (return on capital). And despite the earnings having remained unchanged, due to a reduction in the number of shares outstanding, the EPS (earnings per share) also increases and so dividends can be increased also. And all the while the buisness performance has improved not one iota!

At the next publication of corporate results and at the annual general meeting (AGM) the CEO will point to improving ROE, to improved EPS and to increasing the dividend. He will also allude to the improvement in the share price over the period. And most of the time all of these things have been achieved by way of share-buybacks.

Ask yourself, where is the management skill in any of this?

My ten year old son with no knowledge of corporate management could have embarked on a share repurchase programme and achievedexactly the same result. A robot could have done the same.

Where is the value being added by the C-suite of executives?

In fact, when management embark on a share buy-back programme are they not, in essence, saying that they have no idea how else to deploy capital within the business?

How are they able to justify their fat-cat salaries if they are devoid of ideas on how to take the company forward?

If share repurchases are, in the opinion of the executives, the best use of surplus capital on the balance sheet then that surely does not bode well for the future growth of the business!

Would you want to be invested in such companies?

This is not the end of the story. When a company embarks on a repurchase strategy, it executes that strategy over time rather than buying back shares in a single transaction. And so, each time the management purchases a tranche of its own shares not only will the market price move higher but so too will the PB multiple. The result is that each subsequent share repurchase is at an even more disadvantageous PB multiple than the last, eroding even greater shareholder value!

To make matters worse still, the repurchase is doing nothing more than creating artificial market demand for the shares in the company in which you are invested. The immediate result is that price is pushed higher without a corresponding increase in earnings. This translates into an increase of the PE multiple (and so it will depress the Earnings Yield).

Gradually the price will move ahead of the underlying value of the shares (as discussed in an earlier chapter). Eventually this will lead to a price correction caused by two market influences. First, existing investors may seek to lock in a profit at the overinflated market price and so supply increases. Second, the shares being over priced appear unattractive when compared to other investments and so demand falls away. The price will thus fall back until it reaches an equilibrium where supply and demand are back in balance, said differently when the earnings yield once again looks attractive.
And so what has the executive team achieved for the company and its shareholders over the longer term by deploying a repurchase strategy?

No sustainable share price enhancement, no corporate growth and in fact the destruction of asset and equity value. This is no way to reward long term investors in a business and the only way for a shareholder to benefit from this practice is to jump ship immediately after the buy-back when the price of the shares is temporarily inflated!

Meanwhile, as long term investors are losing, the Chief Executive has announced his retirement and, having cashed in his multi-million dollar bonus, is planning to spend the remainder of his life on the golf-course.

Below is a chart of the Cisco Systems Inc buy-back programme over a five year period which shows how many millions of shares were repurchased.

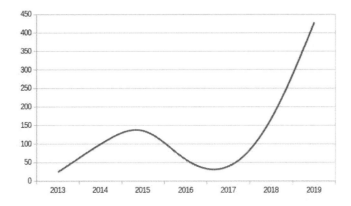

It can be seen that there was a large spike in repurchase activity in 2018 and 2019.

We would expect to see a corresponding spike in the PB multiple, an erosion of equity (book value per share) and a short term price spike which subsequently corrects and falls back in line with the intrinsic value of the shares. And that is exactly what happened.

You will notice that as soon as the spike in buy-back activity dropped off mid-way through 2019 that the share price and PB multiple fell back yet the book value per share had been irreparably diminished.

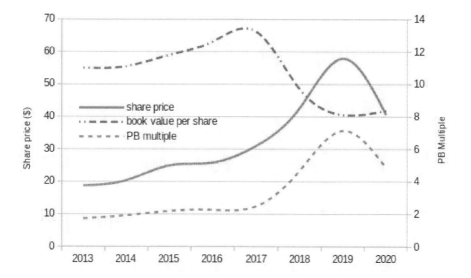

Remember also that when you buy a share in a company you will achieve the Earnings Yield rather than ROE. The situation is no different when the company itself purchases (or repurchases) its own shares.

So if the company is producing a ROE of 15% and invests its capital in growing the business then it would be reasonable to expect it to achieve 15% on the incremental capital being deployed. However, if the same company instead repurchases its own shares at a PB multiple of 3, then it is only achieving an earnings yield of 5% on the same capital!

The company aggressively repurchased its shares pushing the PB all the way up from a little over 2 all the way up to 7. After the aggressive buy-back programme ended the PB multiple subsequently fell back to 4 wiping out approximately 42% of the value of shares repurchased. The price chart below demostrates how Cisco shares purchased by the company for $56 USD early in 2019 subsequently fell back to $37 USD in 2020.

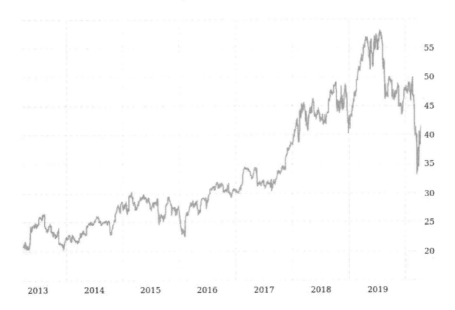

If the management wanted to destroy value it might have been easier to simply burn billions of dollars! But then they would not have qualified for their big bonuses would they.... Silly me!

The situation can be worse still. Some executives borrow to fund the buy-back programme. So not only are they eroding both asset value and equity value for the shareholder, they are also increasing the company's leverage and ladening the shareholders with unnecessary debt.

The argument that CEO's and CFO's make is that they are simply arbitraging the cost of debt capital. Their case may run as follows. If we can borrow at 3%, debt is tax deductable and so the true cost of borrowing is 2.25%, and we can use that money to repurchase shares with an earnings yield of 4.5%.

This argument is flawed. Firstly, a true arbitrage is risk free which this debt for equity swap is not. Secondly, repurchasing shares at premiums to book value de-facto destroys shareholder value and so there is a considerable opportunity cost involved.

Ladening shareholders with increased debt at the same time as destroying shareholder equity will only serve to inflate debt to equity ratios.

Inflated debt to equity ratios will reduce the ability of the company to raise money in future should it be required for genuine business reasons. So the company will be less able to grow during economic booms, and less able to defend itself during economic downturns.

Why would any shareholder want that?

In 2009 the magnitude of the share repurchases at Starbucks, effectively a swap of debt for equity in the capital structure, burned through all of the company's retained earnings and flipped shareholder's equity from a positive $6 billion to a negative $6 billion!

This malpractice is now so out of control that between 2015 and 2020, stock buy-backs and dividends have exceeded corporate profits of S&P500 constituent companies, the balance financed by increasing debt balances. More particularly most of the repurchases have been at PE multiples above 20 implying an earnings yield of less than 5% - a good deployment of capital this is not.

It is difficult for regulators of financial markets to legislate for the malpractice of stock-buybacks because in some circumstances repurchases not only make sense but they are of benefit to shareholders. For example where shares are trading at a discount to book value and the corresponding multiple expansion of the ROE achieved exceeds the marginal return of deploying capital elsewhere. Consequently, shareholders need to wake up and to be active in monitoring, and if necessary to veto, the use of capital for the repurchase of shares by executives where they are not accretive for shareholders.

Warren Buffett favours the use of share-buybacks only if they occur at or below true economic book value. He is, as we all know, one of the best allocators of capital that there is. And so here is a story of what he did when his shares were overvalued.

In 1998 the entire stock market was overpriced and the PB multiple of Berkshire was a little above three when Buffett believed it was worth approximately half of that. So what did he do?

He certainly did not entertain the prospect of buying back his own shares at an over inflated price. No, he is way too shrewd a manager to do that.

Instead he used $22 billion worth of his over priced stock as currency to acquire another company (General Re). Genius!

Buffett effectively acquired the investment portfolio of General Re, which he valued at $25 billion. The portfolio was 90% fixed income products (bonds) which allowed Buffett to switch from a heavy concentration of equity investments in a market that was very over-priced, into much better valued bonds.

And because he thought his stock was being priced by the market at twice its intrinsic value, he effectively paid the equivalent of $11 billion worth of value! Best of all, because he used Berkshire shares as currency for the deal rather than cash he managed to reduce his portfolio exposure to an over priced equity market by half without paying any capital gains tax (then 35%). Even more of a genius!

And there were additional benefits for Berkshire Hathaway such as a large increase in the size of the insurance float, free capital that Buffett likes to use in order to generate returns for his investors.

This highlights the differences between a good allocator of capital and the average executive team, most of whom play in an entirely lower league.

Many senior executives will justify the share repurchases as equivalent to dividends in so far as they are a mechanism for returning capital to shareholders. This is often not the case as we have learned in this chapter. At best these captains of industry are not adequately skilled in the economics of capital allocation and so are blissfully unaware that they are acting contrary to the interests of their shareholders (read 'incompetent'), at worst they are being disingenuous (read "dishonest").

As a related side issue, if you care to do some digging you will find that many sales of shares by insiders (management) occur in the days immediately following an announcement of a share repurchase program! Call me cynical but this appears to be a huge conflict of interest (not currently deemed to be market abuse and so not prohibited by regulators).

I would like to conclude this topic with a rhetorical question for you to consider. If the average tenure of a chief executive is approximately four years, are they motivated to make decisions to benefit the company and its shareholders for decades to come? Or are they instead motivated by what needs to be done to maximize their own personal fortune by meeting the performance targets specified in their LTIP (Long Term Incentive Plan)? I'll leave you to decide!

This is yet another reason to look for investment targets where the senior management have been in office for some considerable time, perhaps even founders of the business who are committed to the company over the long term. Only then will the interests of the management and of the shareholders be truly aligned. By contrast short term CEOs that come and go, never use their own money to buy shares in the company that they manage and instead cash in free grants of shares as soon as they pass their vesting period can never be said to have their interests aligned with those of the company's shareholders.

Examples of companies that have in the past enjoyed the benefit of excellent long term CEOs include Amazon (Jeff Bezos), Berkshire Hathaway (Warren Buffett), Apple (Steve Jobs), Microsoft (Bill Gates) and Twitter (Jack Dorsey).

Before wrapping up this chapter I would like to warn you about the opposite of share buy-backs which are equally damaging to shareholder value. I refer to prolific share issuance.

Some companies burn through capital at an alarming rate and, even with a great product, struggle to make any profit. A good example is the company Tesla. The company requires several billion dollars of new capital each year which it invariably burns through at a rapid rate before returning to market for further fund raising. Debt is one way to fund the company and we have discussed debt and leverage in another chapter. The other way to raise finance is to issue new shares. This latter course of action serves to dilute existing shareholders thereby reducing their share of equity held.

Watch out for companies that have a reputation for regularly issuing new shares as it will not serve you well as a long-term investor.

Rather ironically, share-buybacks usually occur when the company is doing well and awash with cash. Accordingly, the company buys back shares when they trade at premium. At the same time companies will usually issue new shares to raise capital when they are under duress and in need of more capital, so are selling equity at depressed prices. Sell low and buy high? Ouch!

This is the very opposite of what a good investor would seek to do. Accordingly, this situation does on occasion throw up investment opportunities for a shrewd investors. A good example would be the financial crisis of 2008 after which banks issued new shares to raise capital and there were real bargains to be had.

In any event, the lesson to be learned from this chapter is that for the most part management teams have failed shareholders by pulling the wrong levers at the wrong times.

Instead of borrowing at 2.5% to buy back shares at a 4% earnings yield, why not find an incremental project or acquisition that can yield a more favourable long term return? Increase a line of production at 12% return? Or, buy a business at a 9% earnings yield that has prospects for incremental capital deployment at good returns? Alternatively, continue to increase payouts to shareholders with dividends and let them allocate the capital themselves? Or allow cash to accumulate with hopes of deploying it at more favourable returns at some point in the future when opportunity presents itself?

Unfortunately, most higher returning alternatives require patience. If you are a 63-year old CEO, with two-years until retirement, the last thing you have is patience. Get the stock up, get your options in the money, and ride away into the sunset.

Ultimately companies that do not allocate capital well and those that attempt to boost returns by taking on too much leverage, will struggle to compete. Survival of the fittest in economic terms means that some will die and those remaining will thrive. Your job as an investor is to be able to discern one type from the other.

DON'T WRITE ME OFF JUST YET!

Chapter Twenty-One

S hareholder returns often fail to achieve the anticipated ROE. Why should this be?

One of the primary reasons is that the ROE that you see is not the ROE that you get.

Management will often choose to write-off or to write-down the value of its non-performing assets. The former is the removal of the entire value of the asset from the balance sheet, while the latter is a reduction in the book value of the asset.

When an asset is written-down or written-off, we are told that it is a mere "accounting adjustment", a one-off extraordinary cost that should be disregarded. But the fact remains that it reflects the poor outcome of a prior allocation of capital.

If management pay a fancy price in an acquisition, or overpay to develop assets, and the future profits are not high enough to produce adequate returns on invested capital, then management need to be held to account.

Management will attempt to write-off these assets so that prospective returns on remaining assets, and so also on equity, appear more healthy than would otherwise be the case.

This is nothing more than cheating shareholders.

Writing-off assets is like burning shareholder money. As the value of assets reduces, so too does the value of shareholder equity on the other side of the Balance Sheet (Equity = Assets less Liabilities).

It may surprise you to learn that for the S&P500 constituents write-offs and write-downs amount to between 10% - 15% of total earnings each year.

Between 1999 and 2019 cumulative earnings of the S&P500 were $13.5 trillion. In the same period write-offs and write-downs were $1.84 trillion (13.6%).

Write-offs and write-downs typically increase during a downturn in profits when management try to disguise the negative impact of the write-down in a set of already disappointing results. When it's already bad, who cares about more bad news? Just layer it on and tell your investors that these are one-off expenses.

The problem is made worse because not only is shareholder value being eroded, but profitability ratios such as ROE are made to look more favourable than they actually are.

It is not uncommon for executives, and even stock market analysts, to publish operating earnings from the income statement before write-offs and write-downs are taken as an expense, but then they capitalise those inflated profits against understated balance sheet numbers for assets and equity values after write-offs and write-downs! So we end up with an increased numerator over a decreased denominator resulting in overstated ROE, ROA and ROC metrics. It is a complete scandal so be warned!

And so this is a good reason why shareholders fail to achieve their anticipated return. The published ROE number was always pure fantasy.

And so if write-offs and write-downs account for up to 15% of earnings each year, the overstated ROE would need to be reduced by the same amount. A 20% ROE therefore becomes 17%, a 10% ROE becomes 8.5%.

Not all companies engage in this deceptive behaviour, but many do as was highlighted by the 10%-15% of the entire S&P500 earnings being written down every year.

Rex Tillerson, ex-CEO of oil giant Exxon Mobil, once came under pressure to write-off non performing assets. He categorically refused to do so stating that the company needs to earn returns on all of its investments and that the management needs to be held accountable for its allocation of capital. He said that if the company paid a price to put an asset on its books then those assets stay on the books.

If only all corporate executives had such integrity the world of investing would be a better place!

Accordingly, be sure to look out for write-offs and write-downs in the corporate reports and when you see them make adjustments accordingly.

In the course of your analysis, if earnings are quoted before write-offs and write-downs then ensure that you add back the value of the write-offs and write-downs to the balance sheet numbers so that your profitability ratios are a reflection of reality. The data that you use for your analysis must always be economically realistic and conservative.

The lesson to be learned here is not to take financial data at face value when analysing an investment. This topic will be explored in greater detail in the next chapter.

ALL THAT GLITTERS IS NOT GOLD

Chapter Twenty-Two

D ata for corporate entities are everywhere. We live in times where the internet has opened up the world of information and, at the same time, enabled almost any-body to publish almost anything – consequently an investor must exercise a great deal of caution in relation to which data to rely upon.

There are a multitude of share-trading websites, some offered free of charge while others operate on a subscription basis. Stockbrokers also publish data online, ostensibly to make it easier for their clients to make investment decisions.

Please be warned that these data providers are themselves businesses. The share trading websites want to sell subscription services; the free services want to sell advertising by increasing their user base; and the stockbrokers want you to pay commissions by trading more frequently. None is concerned about whether your investments succeed or fail.

The result is that there is little or no quality control around the data being published. I have seen erroneous data time and time again, notified the data provider of the issue and it is rarely if ever corrected.

Some of these errors are obvious, others more subtle and diffi-cult to spot. For example I once spotted a data provider show-ing a company to be paying a dividend yield of 125% (wow, that would be the ultimate investment – the real figure was closer to 3%). I have seen Price to Sales multiples that do not correspond to the Earnings Yield and Net Margin figures quoted, although all three metrics are inextricably related.

Even if the data are free from errors, how confident are you in the methodology used for arriving at each number?

Consider for a moment publication of a PE multiple. Some data providers will calculate this ratio by dividing the market price by historic earnings, while others will use forecast future earn-ings as the denominator. If historic earnings are used some will take the most recent quarter multiplied by four (ignoring cyc-licality); some will take the figure in the most recent annual reports (which could be almost one year out of date); and some will take the trailing twelve months (TTM). Those that use forecast future earnings have even more latitude for deviation based on forecasting methodologies.

As an investor you need to appreciate that these nuances exist and can make an enormous difference.

I could go on, but I think that I have made the point.

The lesson to be learned here is that an investor cannot rely upon data published by third parties, even if the publisher is well respected (for example the Financial Times or the Wall Street Journal).

Ultimately, the only way to ensure that you have the correct investment metrics is to take raw data, preferably from source (the company's annual or quarterly reports), and then to calcu-late the metrics yourself.

This is my preferred approach.

However, one cannot rely on raw data either without making some adjustments.

Why should this be the case?

First, please understand that:

1. Company reports, which include statutory accounts, are first and foremost produced to allow the authorities to ascertain how much tax liability has accrued. As such the formatting of the accounts is designed to mitigate tax liabilities and so is often very misleading for stock-market investors. So, adjustments need to be made.

2. Management often manipulate data in order to suit their specific needs, sometimes to make their poor performance appear better than it is. As the Americans like to say, '*you can put lipstick on a pig but underneath it's still a pig!*' As an investor you need to be able to spot the pigs in order to avoid them.

Some of the things to look out for include share-buybacks, write-offs and write-downs of assets, and flawed assumptions relating to defined benefit pension plans and health liabilities.

The trouble with pensions is that assumptions about investment returns have been too high for too long. This means that too little in the way of pension contributions has been made by the company over time - boosting short term earnings. However, eventually the company will be required to fill the pensions gap and so this will create a substantial capital liability which needs to be considered when adjusting balance sheet numbers.

All of these will invariably lead to earnings being overstated and so in need of being revised downward.

Another might be where the PB multiple, ROE, ROA and ROC are based on understated asset values that are carried at historical cost rather than at replacement values.

Conversely, upward adjustments to earnings include adding back non-cash accounting costs including amortisation of non-decaying intangible assets and goodwill (more on this later).

There are many examples that I could provide of things to look out for in corporate reports, but one of the most important to appreciate is the difference between the capitalisation and expensing of the cost of assets.

Currency: GBP (£)	Company A		Company B	
'000s	Year 1	Year 2	Year 1	Year 2
PROFITABILITY RATIOS				
ROE	19.8%	17.1%	10.8%	22.8%
ROA	10.6%	9.0%	5.4%	11.4%
ROC	15.7%	13.4%	8.3%	17.5%
Profit Margin	22.8%	18.8%	10.8%	22.8%
VALUATION METRICS				
PE	10.53	12.77	22.22	10.53
PS	2.40	2.40	2.40	2.40
PB	2.09	2.18	2.40	2.40
EBITDA	300	300	150	300
EV/EBITDA	9	9	18	9
LEVERGE RATIO				
Long Term Debt/Equity	26.1%	27.3%	30.0%	30.0%

Take a look at the table above.

Which company do you prefer as an investment target?

Would it surprise you to learn that Company A and Company B are in fact the same company?

The only difference is the accounting methodology adopted.

Company A is an example of asset costs being capitalised while Company B is an example of asset costs being expensed– everything else is identical (see table below).

Currency: GBP (£) '000s	Company A		Company B	
	Year 1	Year2	Year 1	Year2
INCOME STATEMENT				
Sales	1,000	1,000	1,000	1,000
COGS	600	600	600	600
Gross Profit	400	400	400	400
OPEX	100	150	250	100
Operating Profit	300	250	150	300
Interest (5%)	15	15	15	15
Tax (20%)	57	47	27	57
Net Earnings	228	188	108	228
BALANCE SHEET				
Assets (total)	2,150	2,100	2,000	2,000
Debt	300	300	300	300
Liabilities (total)	1,000	1,000	1,000	1,000
Equity (Book Value)	1,150	1,100	1,000	1,000
CASH FLOW				
Net income	228	188	108	228
Depreciation	0	50	0	0
Operating Cash Flow	228	238	108	228
CAPEX	150	0	0	0
Investment Cash Flow	150	0	0	0
Net Cash Flow	78	238	108	228
PROFITABILITY RATIOS				
ROE	19.8%	17.1%	10.8%	22.8%
ROA	10.6%	9.0%	5.4%	11.4%
ROC	15.7%	13.4%	8.3%	17.5%
Profit Margin	22.8%	18.8%	10.8%	22.8%
VALUATION METRICS				
PE	10.53	12.77	22.22	10.53
PS	2.40	2.40	2.40	2.40
PB	2.09	2.18	2.40	2.40
EBITDA	300	300	150	300
EV/EBITDA	9	9	18	9
LEVERGE RATIO				
Long Term Debt/Equity	26.1%	27.3%	30.0%	30.0%

You will note that Sales, Cost of Goods Sold (COGS) and Gross Profit are identical in the Income Statement. From that point onwards everything changes in the numbers which has a profound affect on profitability ratios, valuation metrics (except the PS multiple) and even on the leverage ratios.

So in this example, the company has made an investment of $150,000 in some new equipment. Allow me to explain how the accounting treatment of that investment makes such a huge difference in the numbers.

Company A - the capitalisation path. The investment (Capital Expenditure or CAPEX) is treated as an asset on the Balance Sheet – you can see the $150 increase in Assets in Year 1 and a record of the expenditure on the Cash Flow Statement under CAPEX. The asset is subject to depreciation in subsequent years beginning the year following the date on which the item is purchased. (here at a rate of $50 per year over 3 years) – and so the value of the asset is reduced by that amount on the Balance Sheet each subsequent year until its value is depleted. The depreciation becomes an operating cost on the Income Statement as you will see in Year 2 and it is added back as a non-cash expense in the Cash Flow Statement. This serves to boost earnings numbers in the short term but with a drop off in subsequent years. The result is that from Year 1 to Year 2 the profit margin and the profitability ratios all look, on the face of it, to have deteriorated. At the same time the PE multiple increases giving the impression that the shares are worse value than they had been a year earlier relative to the profitability ratios.

Company B - the expensing path. So it recorded the entire $150 cost as an operating expense on the Income Statement, keeping it off-balance sheet. The result is lower earnings in Year 1 (which helps to mitigate tax liabilities) and a big jump in earnings from Year 2. Profitability ratios all jump significantly in Year 2, as does the profit margin, while the PE multiple drops significantly. This gives the appearance that the shares are an excellent value investment.

How strange it is that the same company can appear to an investor to be so different based merely on the accounting approach adopted. But so it is.

There is nothing wrong, per se, with either approach and there may be genuine reasons for preferring one over another.

For example, a company will capitalise costs if it wants to better align the cost of the asset with the revenue that it produces over a number of years.

Alternatively, if the company has a large sum of extraordinary income in a particular year, perhaps it disposed of an under-performing division of the business by selling it, then it faces a large tax liability on that income. Instead it may choose to utilise the income for the purpose of acquiring new capital assets and expensing them immediately to reduce its short term tax liability.

The decision on which accounting methodology to use may also be influenced by a self-serving CEO. For example, a CEO nearing retirement may capitalise costs to boost short term earnings in order to qualify for a big bonus.

Alternatively, if a new management team is brought in to recover an under-performing business then the new CEO may seek to invest heavily, to expense the cost immediately and to blame the short term drop in earnings on the prior management team. He will then claim the glory in subsequent years when profit margins, profitability ratios and earnings leap ahead.

So remember that CEOs and CFOs are in business to make money, for themselves for sure and preferably also for the shareholders. So look out for manipulated data and take nothing for granted.

Earnings and balance sheet manipulation can on occasion be excessive and so tantamount to fraud. That is beyond the scope of this book but if you are interested in learning more then look up as case studies the demise of Worldcom Inc and the far more complicated case of Enron Inc.

And so it follows, that if the same company can appear in an entirely different light based on its accounting approach, comparing two different companies each with different accounting methodologies can be even more difficult.

As such, you cannot take the published data at face value. Instead You will need to normalise the data before it becomes useful. Sometimes the company itself offers adjusted numbers but even then you ought to go further.

It is rather odd that the management of a public company has a fiduciary duty towards investors, its shareholders, but almost never prepares financial data in a format that is of any use to those investors.

The only exception that I have ever seen is Berkshire Hathaway. Warren Buffett publishes financial data in a format in which he would like to see it himself. If only every company was as diligent as Berkshire Hathaway the life of the investor would be so much more straight forward.

However, since we are not living in a utopian world we need to determine what needs to be done to the data that we have available to us.

One course of action that you ought to take is to look at moving averages of a data set rather than looking at a snap-shot.

I have extended the data in the table above over a longer period and taken a four year average which you will note has removed much of the volatility. Now you have a longer term PE multiple and longer term profitability ratios which are far more reliable. Now Company A and Company B look very similar.

This example has a static top line indicating no growth over the period, however for a company with a growing top and bottom line you will need to calculate the growth rate and adjust your averages accordingly to give you a realistic number to use for your analysis.

Currency: GBP (£) 000s	Company A					Company B				
	Year 1	Year 2	Year 3	Year 4	Average	Year 1	Year 2	Year 3	Year 4	Average
INCOME STATEMENT										
Sales	1,000	1,000	1,000	1,000	1,000	1,000	1,000	1,000	1,000	1,000
COGS	600	600	600	600	600	600	600	600	600	600
Gross Profit	400	400	400	400	400	400	400	400	400	400
OPEX	100	150	150	150	138	250	100	100	100	138
Operating Profit	300	250	250	250	263	150	300	300	300	263
Interest (5%)	15	15	15	15	15	15	15	15	15	15
Tax (20%)	57	47	47	47	50	27	57	57	57	50
Net Earnings	228	188	188	188	198	108	228	228	228	198
BALANCE SHEET										
Assets (total)	2,150	2,100	2,050	2,000	2,075	2,000	2,000	2,000	2,000	2,000
Debt	300	300	300	300	300	300	300	300	300	300
Liabilities (total)	1,000	1,000	1,000	1,000	1,000	1,000	1,000	1,000	1,000	1,000
Equity (Book Value)	1,150	1,100	1,050	1,000	1,075	1,000	1,000	1,000	1,000	1,000
CASH FLOW										
Net income	228	188	188	188	198	108	228	228	228	198
Depreciation	0	50	50	50	38	0	0	0	0	0
Operating Cash Flow	228	238	238	238	236	108	228	228	228	198
CAPEX	150	0	0	0	38	0	0	0	0	0
Investment Cash Flow	150	0	0	0	38	0	0	0	0	0
Net Cash Flow	78	238	238	238	198	108	228	228	228	198
PROFITABILITY RATIOS										
ROE	19.8%	17.1%	17.9%	18.8%	18.4%	10.8%	22.8%	22.8%	22.8%	19.8%
ROA	10.6%	9.0%	9.2%	9.4%	9.5%	5.4%	11.4%	11.4%	11.4%	9.9%
ROC	15.7%	13.4%	13.9%	14.5%	14.4%	8.3%	17.5%	17.5%	17.5%	15.2%
Profit Margin	22.8%	18.8%	18.8%	18.8%	19.8%	10.8%	22.8%	22.8%	22.8%	19.8%
VALUATION METRICS										
PE	10.53	12.77	12.77	12.77	12.12	22.22	10.53	10.53	10.53	12.12
PS	2.40	2.40	2.40	2.40	2.40	2.40	2.40	2.40	2.40	2.40
PB	2.09	2.18	2.29	2.40	2.23	2.40	2.40	2.40	2.40	2.40
EBITDA	300	300	300	300	300	150	300	300	300	262.5
EV/EBITDA	9	9	9	9	9	18	9	9	9	10.29
LEVERGE RATIO										
Long Term Debt/Equity	26.1%	27.3%	28.6%	30.0%	27.9%	30.0%	30.0%	30.0%	30.0%	30.0%

When analysing data in this way, some red flags to look out for include:

• On the balance sheet compare the ratio of depreciating assets to total assets – if this ratio is increasing it indicates that the company is capitalising more costs over time;

• On the income statement compare the ratio of amortisation expenses to revenue – if this is decreasing then the company may be spreading amortisation over an extended period to reduce costs in order to boost the bottom line. Companies have discretion when it comes to amortisation and although guidance suggests that amortisation (and depreciation) occur over the useful life of the asset, this is not always the case;

• Calculate months of amortisation by dividing verge assets by amortisation expense and multiply by 12. Again this shows whether the amortisation period is changing;

• On the cash flow statement look at the gap between Net Income and Cash Flow from Operations. The more aggressive the capitalisation the bigger the gap.

• Look out for material changes in the use of working capital over time relative to sales. This can indicate whether a business is improving or deteriorating.

• Compare to industry peers. If a company capitalises expenses which its competitors expense, this may indicate a deviation from best practice in the industry.

So far we have considered the capitalisation of assets, but the same is true for liabilities also.

Off-balance sheet liabilities, namely those that are expensed rather than capitalised, can be problematic because they are often recurring commitments and so unavoidable costs that may sink a business during a downturn if revenue drops.

It is difficult to manage what is not being measured and keeping liabilities off the balance sheet takes them off the radar.

Until recently operating leases were a good example of an off-balance sheet liability however from 2019 accounting rules changed and so these must now be capitalised. Now investors will gain a better understanding of the use of debt in the business. Look out for other off-balance sheet liabilities.

If you have completed your due diligence and are comfortable that the management are not massaging the numbers, you will want to continue your analysis to assess the intrinsic value of the company in order to ascertain whether or not it is a value investment opportunity.

This will require you having to normalise data. Look for extraordinary income or expenditure which will not be repeated in future and so ought to be removed from analysis. For example if a company sold an under-performing part of the business then the proceeds of sale count as earnings but such a boost to earnings can be misleading for an investor. Since the boost would not be repeated in subsequent years after you have invested you ought to exclude it for the purpose of evaluating likely future returns from your investment.

Similarly, the company may have reaped the benefit of a tax break as was the case in the US after Donald Trump became president and reduced the corporate tax rate from 35% to 21%. The stock-market rallied after Trump came to power not because financiers believed that he would be a wonderful president but because every company had a 21.5% boost to net earnings making them immediately more valuable.

A clever political move from Mr Trump as all the newspapers interpreted the Trump stock market rally as a vote of confidence in the new president from Wall Street! And Joe Public bought the story!

However, a boost to earnings brought about by a tax credit is not something for which the management of the company deserves any credit. Again this should be discounted, at least from qualitative analysis.

On the quantitative side, much of that 21.5% gain will eventually be competed away and, at sometime in the future, tax rates may move back up again having the opposite affect on corporate earnings. All of this needs to be considered.

Let us consider Walmart Inc. The figures provided by Walmart are calculated using GAAP (Generally Accepted Accounting Principles). It also publishes, on a voluntary basis, non-GAAP numbers in its reports (not all companies will do this). Where adjusted numbers are published there will be a reconciliation of GAAP versus non-GAAP figures somewhere in the report explaining what has been included or excluded in the adjusted numbers.

For the 2017 fiscal year Walmart reported GAAP Earnings per Share (EPS) of $3.28 against a share price of $86.92 resulting in a PE multiple of 26.50.

This PE multiple, using headline numbers from the quarterly report, was published by most of the online data providers and in stock-brokers literature.

"So what?" I hear you say.

Well a PE multiple of 26.5 is high. It implies an earnings yield of only 3.77%. You may have seen that number and decided not to analyse the company any further.

However, Walmart's adjusted EPS, also in its quarterly report, was in fact $4.42. Now if you calculate the PE multiple you find that it is a much more palatable 19.66 (an implied earnings yield of more than 5%). More interesting but still unlikely to satisfy an investors hurdle rate.

However, that is not the end of the story. Earnings, also known as profit, can be measured in a variety of ways.

Operating earnings measure income from core business activity, namely the selling of goods and services. It excludes unusual or non-recurring items such as merger and acquisition activity, financing costs, redundancy payouts, write-offs and write-downs.)

Reported earnings measure income from continuing operations, and are sometimes referred to as GAAP earnings (Generally Accepted Accounting Principles). These are after write-offs and write-downs.

As discussed in prior chapters, the management has incentives, often related to their compensation, to make profits and profit margins look as healthy as possible. As such, they often publish pro-forma earnings in order to flatter results.

Pro-forma earnings exclude all kinds of expenses such as non-recurring items and non-cash items (depreciation and share based compensation are examples). Essentially, pro-forma earnings more closely resemble cash flow than earnings and so are almost always higher than Reported earnings.

For an investor embarking on analysis none of these measures are of very much use out of the box. It is important to start with reported earnings and then to make a variety of adjustments, both upwards and downward, in an effort to reflect economic reality. You are attempting to properly measure economic profitability and also the amount of capital employed in a business. Do not be surprised if your earnings number ends up being materially different from the company's published numbers – this is normal.

The calculation should run broadly on the basis of the following flow diagram:

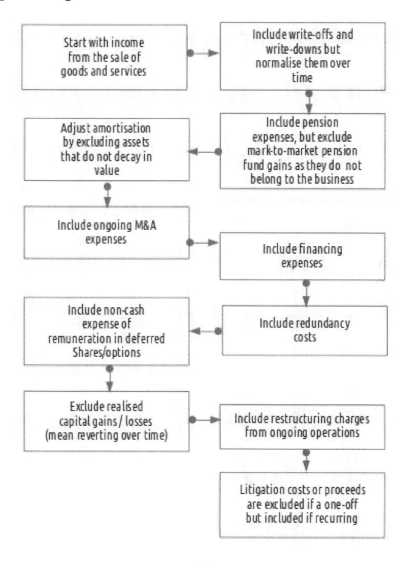

As already mentioned, the statutory accounts are formulated with tax liabilities in mind. Depreciation and amortisation of assets are both tax deductible for example and so on the Income Statement these will be listed as a cost of the business and so subtracted from revenue in order to arrive at Net Income.

Both depreciation and amortisation are non-cash items. Said differently, they are an accounting cost not a physical cost each year. As such, the investor ought to add these back to Net Earnings to give a better reflection of the actual economic earnings of the company.

Similarly, net capital expenditure (CAPEX) is the cost of maintaining the business assets required to keep the business ticking and so this is a cost, which is not accounted for in the income statement, which reduces the earnings of the shareholders of the business. So deduct CAPEX from reported earnings in your calculation.

CAPEX, found in the Cash Flow Statement, is capitalised on the Balance Sheet and charged to the Income Statement incrementally over an extended period by way of depreciation or amortisation of the asset.

Finally, changes in Working Capital need to be factored in to the equation. If working capital increased over the period then it will be a positive number and so enhance Owner Earnings, if working capital decreased then it will be a negative number and so diminish Owner Earnings. All of the following will have a bearing on working capital: deferred income taxes; loss on extinguishment of debt; accrued liabilities; accounts payable; receivables; and, one off movements of cash from the disposal of assets, acquisition of businesses and other investing activities.

Only by performing these calculations is it possible to understand how much money the business has actually generated for its shareholders.

Warren Buffett uses what he terms "Owner Earnings" when analysing companies and this is a similar concept.

Internal growth requires a company to generate free cash flow or cash after maintenance capital expenditures (CAPEX) and distributions to shareholders. That cash is the fuel of growth. And so Owner Earnings is essentially a measure of the ability of the company to grow.

Conversely, companies that are unable to generate positive free cash flow will continually require debt or new equity capital and will not earn an acceptable return on capital for a long term investor.

The name of the game is to buy a fast growing company at a discount to intrinsic value. Over the longer term the price of the share will compound at a rate equal to the growth rate of the business plus accretion back to fair value as an added boost to the profitability of your investment portfolio (see Appendix Two).

So, back to Walmart and a look at the accounts published for the fiscal year ended 31 January 2018.

Net Income	$10,523m
Add back Depreciation, Depletion, Amortisation and certain other non-cash charges.	+ $10,529m
Add back or subtract, as appropriate, Changes in Working Capital	+ $7,898m
Subtract net CAPEX	- $9,673m
Owner earnings	$19,277m

It should be noted that in relation to intangible assets, those that are non-economic costs, said differently those that do not decay in value, should not be amortised. Where there is evidence that they have been amortised an adjustment needs to be made by the equity investor. Goodwill, trademarks, trade names and customer relationships lose little, if any, economic value over time.

While it may be tax advantageous to amortise a non-decaying intangible assets, for the investor there will be no CAPEX required to maintain the earnings power of the asset and so that amortisation charge is added back.

Companies deal with intellectual property (patents, trademarks, etc.) in a variety of strategic ways. Consider the company Coca-Cola as a wonderful example. Its management decided not to patent its special recipe, opting instead to trademark the name and to keep the formula as an unprotected "corporate secret."

A patent would have expired after 20 years and the recipe would have then been in the public domain for any other company to copy. So, had they taken the patent route then the intangible asset that is the formula would have decayed in terms of losing earnings power for the business and so quite rightly would have been amortised over time. In the event as a corporate secret the same recipe became a non-decaying intangible asset that continues to generate earnings for the company more than 100 years later.

Another example is when Berkshire Hathaway acquired See's Candy, it carried $36m of goodwill from the acquisition on its balance sheet. GAAP accounting then required that goodwill be amortised over a period of not more than 40 years, so Berkshire

Hathaway decided to amortise it at a rate of $1m per year for 36 years.

From an accounting standpoint See's Candy is gradually losing its goodwill value. However, in reality the economic goodwill assignable to See's Candy will not decline at all for Berkshire Hathaway in terms of earnings power but, given good management, will in fact increase.

In 1983, See's Candy earned about $27 million pre-tax on $11 million of net operating assets. By 1995 it earned $50 million on $5 million of net operating assets. Clearly See's economic goodwill had increased dramatically over time. Just as clearly, See's Candy was worth many hundreds of millions of dollars more than its stated value on Berkshire's books.

Enough said about non-decaying intangible assets.

Moving on to assets that do decay in value (both tangible and intangible), these are as real a cost to the business as any other. These assets need to be renewed, said differently capital expenditure (CAPEX) will be needed in order to maintain those assets.

Patents and intellectual property pertaining to R&D (research and development) investment are good examples of decaying intangible assets.

When calculating Owner Earnings on decaying assets it is important not to double count the maintenance cost. It is for this reason that when calculating cash flows, we add back legitimate amortisation and depreciation and then subtract CAPEX. While the management has a wide discretion over the way it books depreciation and amortisation, it has no such latitude when it comes to maintenance CAPEX. As such, CAPEX is a more reliable indicator of maintenance costs.

Note also that if CAPEX less depreciation and amortisation is negative, then assets are arguably not being properly maintained which could result in trouble further down the road. Conversely, if CAPEX exceeds depreciation and amortisation then that indicates growth and expansion as the management are investing greater sums of money on infrastructure.

Before moving on, one word of warning: Investors are often led astray by CEOs and equity analysts who equate depreciation charges with the amortization charges we have just discussed. In no way are the two the same: With rare exceptions, depreciation is an economic cost every bit as real as wages, materials, or taxes.

Accordingly EBITDA (earnings before interest, taxes, depreciation and amortization) is not, in the eyes of a value investor, a meaningful measure of performance. Managements that dismiss the importance of depreciation - and emphasise EBITDA which is a cash flow metric - are likely to make flawed decisions. You ought to bare this in mind when reading company reports and before making investment decisions. (More on EBITDA later).

In any event, I seem to have digressed, let us return to our analysis of Walmart.

We calculated Owner Earnings of $19,277m and we know that there were 2,995m shares outstanding at the relevant time (as stated in the annual report) and so the Owner Earnings per Share were $6.43.

Now using the $86.92 share price again, we arrive at a PE multiple is 13.50 (implied earnings yield of 7.4%). This now looks like a very interesting investment opportunity and far better than the misleading PE multiple of 26.5 displaying on so many financial websites.

In the 21 months that followed this analysis the Walmart share price advanced 39.5% from the $86.92 to $121.28 on 16th December 2019, and so it was indeed a good value investment as our calculations had revealed. Lucky we refused to base our trading decision on the misleading PE multiple of 26.5 published in the newspapers and online!

And so once again we see that stock-market investing requires quite some work on the part of the investor. Calculate the true earnings that the company generates for its owners rather than taking numbers that are reported pursuant to accounting principles which invariably change from time-to-time or from jurisdiction-to-jurisdiction.

> *"...we much prefer to purchase $2 of earnings that is not reportable ... under standard accounting principles than to purchase $1 of earnings that is reportable." Warren Buffett*

Although the owner earnings worked out higher and more favourable in our analysis of Walmart, often it goes the other way and the actual investor numbers are in fact less favourable. In such circumstances performing these calculations may help you to avoid investing in the wrong company.

Calculating investing metrics manually is the only way to make an informed decision about where to invest your money. Perhaps now you are starting to appreciate why good active fund managers charge a fee for all of the work that they do.

Hopefully you will also now treat the financial metrics published in the newspapers or on the internet or by your stockbrokers with extreme caution.

With reference to Owner earnings it should be noted Buffett estimates both the Capex and Changes in Working Capital required to maintain the company's long-term competitive position. This may be different from the Capex and Changes to Working Capital in a company's cash flow statement.

Ultimately, many of these things are subjective and you will need to take an informed view. Even if your numbers are not exactly the same as the next analyst, having performed the requisite adjustments on published data will stand you in good stead as an investor. You will certainly be a long way ahead of investors who do not perform this kind of analysis.

Adjusted earnings numbers will highlight issues with the company.

For example if the sum of CAPEX expenditure plus negative changes in working capital exceed the depreciation, depletion and amortisation number then this is evidence that the company is having to spend more simply to maintain its existing competitive standing. Eventually the company will burn through cash, require new injections of capital or else perhaps it will simply go 'pop'. This situation will result in adjusted earnings being lower than published Net Income.

However, an adjusted earnings number that exceeds the Net Income figure is indicative of a sustainable company with surplus capacity to grow, Said differently, the company is utilising less capital to sustain itself and to grow than it is earning – the difference being gains for the benefit of the shareholders either in the form of dividends or else growth in the equity value of the businesses.

Adjusted earnings will help you to arrive at a reliable PE multiple (often very different from published numbers). In this way you may formulate an opinion on the extent to which it may be under-priced, or not as the case may be.

By way of example, if the company is trading on a PE multiple of 12 and you believe that it ought to be valued closer to a 15 multiple, then the stock is trading at only 80% of its intrinsic value. The gap will invariably close as price tends towards intrinsic value. This will not happen immediately, but over some period of time. So, it is reasonable for you to assume that there will be a 25% accretion of the price to intrinsic value over your holding period [If valued at 80% of intrinsic value, after having closed the 20% gap the share price will have increased by 25% (20/80)].

> *"In the short run the stock market acts like a voting machine reflecting all kinds of irrational attitudes and expectations, while functioning in the long run more like a weighing machine reflecting a firm's true value." Warren Buffett*

Since we are long term value investors we work on the basis of a notional 10 year holding period which implies that, on average, an extra 2.5% will be added to each of your annual returns.

Since you have ascertained that the shares are currently trading on a PE multiple of 12, which in turn implies an earnings yield of 8.5% per annum, we are able to add this to your 2.5% annual value accretion which suggests that you ought to expect an average 11% annual return over your holding period. Compounding at this rate means doubling your money in little over six years. Not bad!

Be reminded that we are interested in ascertaining value based on analysis of a range of probable outcomes rather than trying to find a magic formula.

So no valuation technique should be run in isolation, but instead ought to be run in parallel with other valuation simulations. This is known as Monte Carlo analysis. By comparing the output of each simulation it is possible to determine, with a degree of confidence, the most likely outcome.

So another simulation that you might like to run along side this PE multiple technique is that described earlier where it was explained how Earnings Yields gravitate towards ROE over the long term.

DEBT, A FRIEND OR A FOE?

Chapter Twenty-Three

I f you are able to generate a good return on capital, then it stands to reason that if you are able to boost the capital at your disposal then your returns will be magnified. This is the premise for using leverage.

In an everyday context many of us use leverage to buy the home that we live in by way of granting a mortgage over the property in favour of the lender.

So, imagine buying a property for $100,000 with cash. After one year the property market rises 10%. The market price of your property is now $110,000 and so you have a mark-to-market gain of $10,000 – perfectly straight forward.

Now imagine that you had instead bought a property for $1m using the same $100,000 cash and that you had borrowed the $900,000 difference at an annual rate of 5%. After one year the property market has risen by the same 10% so that your property is now commanding a price tag of $1.1m. Your mark-to-market gain is now $100,000 less the interest on the debt of $45,000. With the use of leverage you have increased your earnings from $10,000 to $55,000.

So far so good!

However, imagine the same scenarios above but this time the market declines by 10% in value over the year.

As an unlevered buyer you will have seen your property fall in price to $90,000. You will have a mark-to-market loss of $10,000.

But as a debt laden buyer you would have seen your property fall in value to $900,000. The debt is still $900,000 and so the $100,000 equity value that you once had has been completely wiped out. To make matters worse not only do you still owe the bank $900,000 in debt but you also owe $45,000 in accrued interest. You are de-facto bankrupt!

In good times an over-leveraged company can do very well, but in bad times they can go bust.

> *"It's only when the tide goes out that you learn who's been swimming naked." Warren Buffett*

I believe that this analogy perfectly describes why over lever-aged companies present a high risk for investors and so should be avoided.

They are inherently unstable and the risk versus reward profile makes very little sense.

In our example, had you been a leveraged buyer you would have had the risk of $145,000 to the downside in a bad year versus a gain of $55,000 in a good year. Certainly not odds skewed in your favour.

By contrast, had you been a prudent buyer the risk versus reward were balanced at $10,000 either way – still unattractive for an investor, but preferable to the alternative.

In reality this prudent buyer may be receiving rental yield of 5%, so annual income of $5,000 on the property. So the risk is a capital loss of $10,000 offset by rent of $5,000 (net $5,000 loss) versus a capital gain of $10,000 plus rent of $5,000 (net $15,000 gain). This is now the kind of risk versus reward profile (1:3) that an intelligent investor would admire because the odds are indeed skewed in his favour.

Rental income would have made very little difference to you as a leveraged buyer – you would still be bankrupt!

The better investment opportunity is the one that has less variability and which will still be churning out good returns ten or twenty years from now without any insolvency risk.

> *"We will reject interesting opportunities rather than over-leverage our balance sheet. As one of the Indianapolis "500" [car race] winners said: To finish first, you must first finish." Warren Buffett*

It is just like Aesop's fable about *'the hare and the tortoise'*. The hare may be ahead at the beginning but the tortoise wins in the end. In other words investing is a marathon and not a sprint.

An investor must pay as much attention to avoiding disasters as he does to picking winners. Risk and reward are equally important.

You will recall that ROC is the return on both debt and equity while ROE is the same return rebased against equity alone, ergo the larger the differential between these two metrics the more debt that the company is utilising. If the debt to equity ratio is not immediately available then the difference between ROC and ROE is a perfect proxy. The three metrics are all inextricably linked.

$$(\frac{ROE}{ROC})-1=\frac{Debt}{Equity}=\text{Debt to Equity Ratio}$$

So it follows that if ROC is much lower than ROE then that will be due to a combination of two factors. The first is the use of leverage in the business and the second is where equity is understated on the balance sheet.

If equity (book value) is understated, either because assets are carried at historic cost or due to write-offs and write-downs, then you would get an inflated return on equity. When this is the case then a sizeable differential between ROC and ROE may be justified albeit with the caveat that the ROE number is unreliable. If this occurs in combination with a high PB multiple then that is almost certainly confirmation of understated equity. One final test is the trend of asset and equity values over time. In a growth company they should be rising. In case of write-offs, write-downs and premium share buy-backs they are likely to be reducing. Observe the rate of decrease and whether it is a one-off or a modus operandi.

However, it is the combination of a big difference between the returns with an absolute low return on capital that merits further digging. If ROC is significantly higher than the cost of capital then there is not too much cause for concern, but if ROC is low relative to the cost of capital then that is an issue and merits further digging.

In addition to straightforward debt, the investor must also take into account other forms of debt owed by the company including pension fund deficits and the value of convertible bonds where the likelihood of conversion is small. [Convertible debt is a hybrid fixed income product with an embedded option enabling the bond holder to convert the debt into equity. The option premium that would otherwise be paid by the bond holder is instead used as an offset to reduce the rate payable on the debt. In this way a company is able to reduce its cost of borrowing.]

The more debt that the company carries, the more risk of catastrophe during cyclical downturns.

The debt maturity profile also needs to be considered. If the debt is to be paid back gradually over an extended period then, interest payments aside, the company must be able to meet those obligations regardless of periodic dips in cash flow. However, if the debt requires being paid off in the short term and the debt to earnings ratio is high, then any dip in earnings may result in a debt default, a credit rating downgrade or worse, insolvency.

Investing in a company with a weak balance sheet is dangerous, so also pay attention to the debt to equity ratio which should not be too high. A ratio of one means that the business uses as much debt as it does equity in its business operation. A ratio greater than one and the business is fuelled principally by debt. A figure of less than one is preferable because debt should supplement equity, not vice versa.

Having said this, the liabilities of a company must be seen in the context of the sector in which it operates. Banks and financial institutions are, by definition, very highly leveraged. Prior to the financial crisis of 2008 banks typically had a liability to equity ratio in the low teens. Today tighter regulation requires them to be better capitalised but even then their liabilities to equity ratio will be a relatively high single digit number.

Some companies have such strong cash flows that they are able to grow strongly both organically and by acquisition without any debt at all. These are fantastic companies to invest in.

On the subject of cash flows, please be aware that even the most profitable of companies can go bust if cash flow dries up. Cash flowing for a business is like blood flow for you and me. No matter how healthy you may be, if there is a sudden issue with your blood flow you will end up dead.

Accordingly, you need to be confident that a company has healthy cash flows. So, where a company has debt on its balance sheet you want to look at the interest coverage ratio which measures how many times a company can cover its current interest payment from its earnings. The ratio is calculated by dividing a company's earnings before interest and taxes (EBIT) by the company's interest expenses for the same period.

When a company's interest coverage ratio is 1.5 or lower, its ability to meet interest expenses may be questionable.

Stability in interest coverage ratios is one of the most important things to look for. A declining interest coverage ratio may indicate that a company will be unable to pay its debts in the future. So you need to analyse interest coverage ratios over time in order to provide a clear picture. Trends may emerge which give you a much better idea of whether a low current interest coverage ratio is improving or worsening, or if a high current interest coverage ratio is stable.

Banks and other lenders will often provide debt finance only on condition that the interest coverage ratio is maintained above a prescribed threshold, thereby reducing the risk of default. If a company allows its interest coverage ratio to drop below that threshold the loan may become immediately repayable which could be catastrophic for the company. You will usually find commentary on this from a finance executive in the annual reports of the business.

Also be aware of a mismatch between the structure of the debt and the use of the debt. A company may reduce its interest costs by concentrating its borrowing at short maturities, which are invariably cheaper than long term debt. But how much additional risk is introduced by borrowing short term for the purpose of investing in long-term infrastructure projects? Short term debt will need to be refinanced periodically and if interest rates turn then the initial investment made by the company may be pushed into the unviable territory.

Some investors like to use the Weighted Average Cost of Capital (WACC) to analyse a company. WACC, as the name suggests, is the weighted average of the cost of debt and the cost of equity.

Measuring the debt element of the cost of capital is straightforward, identifiable by the net interest paid by the company.

Measuring the equity element of the cost of capital is far from easy and to all intents of purpose can be no more than a finger in the wind estimate.

Some people use 10% as a proxy for the cost of equity, presumably based on the Ibbotson equity premium over risk free rates.

Others use a CAPM model (Capital Asset Pricing Model) which uses beta as a measure of risk, although this makes very little sense to most value investors:

> *"Beta... implies that a stock that has fallen sharply in value is more risky than it was before it fell. A value investor would argue that a company represents a lower-risk investment after it falls in value." Warren Buffett*

Consequently, the use of WACC is of limited practical value. Cast aside anything that you may have learned while studying for your MBA – text book theory is often best left in the class room!

Consideration must also be given to the cost of capital versus the Return on Capital (ROC). When the ROC falls below the cost of capital the company is losing money. While this may appear to be a statement of the obvious, you would be surprised how many companies borrow money at, for example, 8% and subsequently only generate a 5% return on capital! Bear in mind, however, that interest on debt is tax deductible and so a company with a 25% tax rate paying 8% interest is in fact only paying 6% equivalent.

Even if ROC is marginally higher than the cost of capital there is no margin of safety in the investment. If, for example, interest rates move up, or if ROC declines, then the company may find itself underwater.

As such, look for a significant difference between the ROC and the interest rate paid by the company on debt.

The company can manage its own cost of equity by adjusting its dividend policy and retaining more or less of its earnings as needs require.

While a high debt to equity ratio indicates excessive leverage and little or no spare funding capacity, a low debt to equity ratio evidences spare capacity to fund growth or to weather the next economic storm.

So far we have focused our attention on long term debt. Short term debt also requires analysis.

The current ratio and quick ratio are the tools to be used for this job.

Both measure short-term liquidity of the business, said differently, its ability to generate enough cash to pay off all debts should they become due.

The current ratio of a company is found by dividing its current assets by current liabilities. If all short obligations had to be met immediately (short term debt, accounts payable or accrued liabilities), the current ratio informs us whether they could be covered from the liquid assets of the business.

If the current ratio is less than one, then it owes more than it can raise and this is a red flag in terms of financial risk. The higher the ratio the better.

The quick ratio is more conservative than the current ratio because the numerator in the equation includes only assets that may be liquidated in 90 days (hence the name 'quick') and so excludes less liquid current assets such as inventory. Again you would not want to see a ratio of less than one.

To conclude this chapter I would like to point out that debt is not all bad. You need to understand how debt is being utilised.

Prudent managers use debt only to facilitate cash flows. Exuberant managers utilise debt to leverage the assets of the business in an effort to enhance returns. Incompetent managers swap equity for debt in share buy-backs enhancing the risk profile of the business with no corresponding return.

EBITDA, DA, DA, DA

Chapter Twenty-Four

E BITDA is a peculiar looking acronym which is ubiquitous in the business world. It is most prevalent in the world of mergers and acquisitions but it also has other uses. Let us explore what it is, how it is used and whether it is of any value to an equity investor.

EBITDA stands for *Earnings before Interest, Tax, Depreciation and Amortisation.*

It is, in essence, a cash flow metric which starts with the output of the Income Statement, namely Net Earnings (E), and then adds back capital structure expenses of the business (I&T) and non-cash expenses (D&A).

Adding back D&A is something dealt with in detail in a previous chapter and so I shall not rehearse those arguments again here.

In relation to the I&T element, this makes the metric capital structure neutral. What does this mean?

If I am acquiring another company in its entirety then I am not concerned with the existing capital structure of the business. It may operate with far more debt than I intend to use and so it will pay more interest than I will eventually pay. It may be subject to entirely different tax rates than those that apply to me. As such, I want to know how much in the way of earnings the business will generate for me before tax and interest are accounted for. Only then can I assess the value that the business will bring to me.

It is not uncommon for mergers and acquisitions to be structured at a price which is a multiple of EBITDA.

However, for a stock-market investor the situation is entirely different. The existing capital structure of the business is enormously relevant because it will prevail after an investment is made. Accordingly, EBITDA is far less useful when buying shares.

In fact, it can be misleading for stock-market investors:

- It represents cash flow before considering the depreciation of fixed assets and so discounts the amount of maintenance capital (CAPEX) required to replace those assets over time. Said differently, it ignores the capital intensity of the business. Imagine two companies each with earnings of $1m per year – one of the companies requires capital expenditure each year of $600,000 while the other only requires $100,000 – the latter company represents a better investment as the net earnings will be $900,000 rather than $400,000. You will recall from earlier in the book that we discussed Free Cash Flow and Owner Earnings. Both metrics are of great use to an equity investor and both exclude non-cash expenses such as amortisation and depreciation but then include CAPEX and changes to Working Capital in order to redress the balance. This is where they are are distinguished from EBITDA.

- In relation to the I&T element, an over-leveraged company paying too much interest and with a rising tax rate may experience a rising EBITDA, while Return on Capital is actually declining.

If you are told that a company would have made money had it not had to bear the cost of replacing its decaying assets, paying the bank interest and paying the tax man then you really do not want to invest in that company as a shareholder.

The only feasible use of EBITDA for a stock-market investor is in considering what the company in its entirety may be valued at if it is acquired at some point in the future. If other companies in the sector are valued at perhaps 9x EBITDA then you may be able to estimate a ball-park takeover value. If the company that you are looking to invest in trades at less than that multiple then there may be a chance of a price uplift if a takeover approach is ever made. However, this is entirely speculative and no investment in the shares of a company should be made on this basis.

Think also about this. If you are using a PE multiple and the earnings improve because tax rates reduce or the cost of debt is curtailed, then the PE multiple will fall indicating that the company is now better value than before – which it is. However, if you are using Price/EBITDA, or Enterprise Value (EV)/ EBITDA, then an increase in earnings for the reasons given will bring about no change in EBITDA and so the ratio remains unchanged, despite the business being better value than before!

Long story short, its probably best to ignore EBITDA!

DISCOUNT THE DISCOUNTED CASH FLOW MODEL

Chapter Twenty-Five

A discounted cash flow (DCF) model is the text book methodology for assessing the viability of a financial investment using the concepts of the time value of money.

DCF analysis attempts to figure out the net present value of an investment today, based on projections of how much money it will generate in the future.

At a very basic level if you expect to receive $110 next year and your discount rate is 10% then you would value that future receipt at having a $100 value today. Said differently, $100 is the Net Present Value (NPV) of your future projected cash flow.

For example, if you are able to invest $90 today to produce $110 next year then you are instantly converting $90 into $100 in present value terms. A great investment!

If, however, you had to invest $105 in order to produce $110 next year then that would fail the test of commercial viability because you are effectively converting your $105 into $100 in present value terms. Only a mad man would do that!

This methodology is used all of the time by company executives deciding whether or not to invest in infrastructure, perhaps a new piece of machinery for the factory. In such circumstances a DCF model works perfectly. You know how much the new equipment costs; you know how much the machinery will add to your productivity and the value of the increase in output; you know the life span of the new machinery; and, you know your cost of capital. All of this will enable you to calculate the NPV of the cash flows produced by the investment.

This is where the usefulness of the DCF model ends.

Some people suggest that DCF models may be used to calculate the NPV of a share in a company in order to ascertain whether it is under-priced or over-priced.

I take exception to that suggestion as do many of the greatest stock-market investors. The use of a DCF model for investment purposes is like trying to push a square peg into a round hole. It is simply not fit for purpose.

The issue with DCF modelling for the purpose of share valuations is that they require too many assumptions of unknown quantities.

An investment in shares does not have a finite life. How long will you hold the shares? Most investors are unable to answer this question at the point of purchase. Changing the time variable in a DCF model has enormous implications in terms of the result.

So let us say that for the purpose of populating the input variables for the model you assume that the investment is to be held for ten years, the next challenge is to forecast dividend payments and cash flows for the next ten years. You also need to estimate the terminal value of the shares at the point of exit.

What degree of accuracy do you think you might achieve on any of these assumptions? Forecasting cash flows and earnings ten years out is impossible.

It is difficult to predict dividends for the next two or three years, let alone for years four or five. Ten years forward? Really?

If you change any of the input variables in a DCF model then the output is different by an enormous order of magnitude.

Said differently, several analysts using the same DCF model will each come up with vastly different estimates for the value of a share. So how does the DCF model help anyone?

The suggestion that DCF modelling may be used to ascertain the true value of a share is preposterous.

To make matters worse the DCF model uses the Weight Adjusted Cost of Capital (WACC). This is essentially a weighted average of the cost of equity finance with the cost of debt finance and is fraught with difficulty.

Most analysts assigns a notional 10% to the equity element of the cost of capital, presumably to reflect the long-term Ibbotson risk premium over the prevailing risk free rate.

But here is the rub - the cost of debt is usually less than the cost of equity and so the more debt a company has the lower its WACC will be. This means that a DCF model prefers heavily leveraged companies over those which are prudently well managed with low levels of debt to equity. This is absolutely absurd. Over leveraged companies should be avoided at all costs by a value investor.

Another consideration is that interest rates are constantly changing which has an impact on the discount rate applied in a DCF model. In 2019 the 10-year US Treasury note saw its yield decline from 2.69% to 1.92% (a 29% decline). This had a profound affect on stock prices with the S&P500 chalking up a 31.5% gain in 2019 despite the revenue and profits of its constituent companies averaging 4% gains. And so it can be seen that DCF modelling is entirely unhelpful when it comes to valuing shares.

The best systems for valuing shares will be those that may be applied by any number of people, all of whom will arrive at a similar conclusion.

Although Warren Buffett and his partner Charlie Munger acknowledge that the value of a share is essentially its discounted future cash flows they do not rely on DCF models.

At the annual Berkshire Hathaway meeting of shareholders in 1996, Charlie Munger said that they use a fingers and toes style of valuation. He went on to say that while Buffett refers to discounted cash flows he had never seen him calculate one. Buffett joked in response that there are some things that you only do in private!

What Munger was saying is that if a company is not obviously good value, then the opportunity is not attractive enough. You should not need complicated spread sheets and methodologies to help distinguish a good investment idea from a bad one.

> *"If you see an overweight man walking down the street you do not need to know his weight to conclude that he is fat."* Benjamin Graham

In other words, forget about DCF models. If the value of a company does not scream at you then drop the investment idea.

PART SIX

Brushing up on technique

THERE IS NO ONE SIZE FITS ALL

Chapter Twenty-Six

E ach investor will lean towards different types of invest-ment. Again, there is no magic formula that works for everyone and there is no one-size-fits-all approach to investing.

By way of example let us consider the approach preferred by the legendary investor Benjamin Graham.

Graham sought value investments rather than growth stocks.

He looked for a return based on a revaluation of the share price in line with its intrinsic value. Accordingly his subjective requirements would be very different than those for a growth investor, such as Warren Buffett, or an income investor, such as a pension fund manager.

Graham had a number of pre-requisites before considering an investment for his portfolio. He would look for as many of the following attributes as possible:

- His preference was for large out-of-favour companies as he felt that small companies were too unstable in terms of performance and so too high a risk, although he did acknowledge that this risk could be managed by way of diversification. He would therefore only consider looking at the largest third of businesses in an industry sector. By contrast a growth investor may instead prefer to invest in small companies or mid-caps (middle sized companies) with larger growth prospects.

- He favoured businesses in a strong financial position – those whose current assets are at least twice the value of its current liabilities and whose long-term debt is less than its Net Current Asset Value (NCAV). As previously discussed in this book, a strong balance sheet is of paramount importance when selecting a long term investment, although a short term investor may be less concerned about the balance sheet if a stock looks oversold and so likely to benefit from a short term bounce.

- He liked companies with a consistent dividend policy over an extended period. By contrast a growth investor may prefer no dividend at all because he seeks compounded growth from reinvestment of profits – Amazon and Berkshire Hathaway pay no dividends and have enjoyed meteoric growth.

- He sought businesses which had a PB multiple of not more than 1.5x. However, as discussed earlier in this book, there are sometimes good reasons for the PB multiple to be high, particularly when valuable assets are carried at historical cost rather than at their true economic value. As such this requirement ought to be assessed on a case by case basis depending on the company or the industry sector in which you are considering making an investment.

- He looked for profitability over an uninterrupted ten year period in addition to constant earnings growth over the same time scale. This would remove start-ups or rapidly growing but yet to be profitable companies from his short list. It might also remove a company that legitimately decides to expense infrastructure investment rather than capitalising it. Again this requirement needs to be assessed on a case by case basis. You may prefer to adopt an entirely different approach.

- He wanted a modest PE multiple, typically less than 15x the average of the past three years' earnings and 25x the average over the past seven years. This part will vary from time-to-time as a result of prevailing interest rates. Remember that the reciprocal of the PE multiple is the Earnings Yield. A PE of 15x implies a hurdle rate of 6.66% investor return but if prevailing bank base rates were in the double digits, as they have been, then an investor would seek a better return from equities and so the PE multiple threshold would reduce to something below 10x.

The lesson to be learned here is that you should not attempt to emulate a formula applied by any other successful trader, past or present.

The wonderful thing about the stock-market is that every participant has his own unique set of requirements and so has very different drivers dictating when and what to buy and to sell.

This is also the reason that the market is in a constant state of flux with prices moving almost constantly, and this results in there always being a good investment opportunity for someone!

DIVIDEND POLICY

Chapter Twenty-Seven

---

dividend is a distribution of all or some of the companies profit to its shareholders.

The often quoted Payout Ratio is the percentage of earnings paid out as dividends, the remainder being retained for re-investment in the company.

Some investors, termed 'income investors', seek out companies that pay sizeable dividend yields. Such investors are less concerned with the growth prospects of the company. Examples may be pension fund managers who know that they have a liability to make pension payments on a regular basis and so use the income from their investments to satisfy that obligation. This is know as liability matching investing.

In contrast 'growth investors' seek long term growth and are happy to forgo dividends entirely, or else accept a meagre dividend, in order that earnings be ploughed back into the money making machine that is the business.

You will need to decide which kind of investment style best suits you. This could be a decision that changes over the course of time due to changes in your personal circumstances. If you are young and have an income from another source then long term growth of your wealth might be your priority. However, if you are retired and have already accumulated reasonable wealth throughout your working life then you might prefer regular income from your portfolio in order to supplement your pension.

Many very good companies including Berkshire Hathaway and Amazon Inc. do not pay a dividend but have provided their investors with phenomenal growth and appreciation in value.

In fact Berkshire did pay a dividend once. The only dividend it ever paid to its shareholders was ten cents per share on 3rd January 1967, a mere 0.54% yield on the then $17.87 stock price. The total paid to all shareholders as dividends on that date was $101,755. It may surprise you to learn that had Berkshire not paid that solitary dividend but instead retained the earnings and reinvested the money back in the business it would be worth $3.1 billion today! Such is the power of retained earnings for the long term value investor.

Profits should only be retained and reinvested in a business where the expected rate of return that they will produce justifies their retention. A shareholder ought to be happy to forgo $1 of dividend today in return for significantly more than $1 of extra value tomorrow.

Additionally, where a company retains earnings it invests that money at the existing ROE, but if it pays those earnings out as dividends and the shareholder then decides to reinvest the dividend by buying new shares in the company then that money will only achieve the Earnings Yield. The former is a far better outcome for the investor.

It is therefore more beneficial to the shareholder for a growth company to retain its earnings rather than paying them out.

Said differently, return on incremental capital deployed is even more important than the return on existing capital, and returns on incremental capital is optimised by retention where sufficient opportunity exists to reinvest that capital at existing, or better, rates of return.

It stands to reason that strong companies which are able to produce a healthy return on capital ought to optimise that return by increasing the capital invested in the business. This is best achieved by adding to shareholder equity rather than by taking on additional debt. Retention is therefore the most sensible strategy.

Ergo, where a company pays out most of its earnings as dividends it suggests that the company has little or no opportunity to invest in growth and so this ought to be a red flag to a growth investor.

In reality very few companies possess the re-deployment opportunity for retained profits. Even if a company does possess a nice opportunity to reinvest retained earnings, too few corporate executives possess the skill to invest well. Thus, most companies ought to pay most of their profits as dividends.

Unfortunately most public companies do retain the majority of profit and then go on to squander it.

Many companies will retain earnings and, rather than investing it to achieve a healthy ROE, they will instead use it to buy-back its own stock. Doing so is no different from you and me buying stock in the company – it achieves the Earnings Yield rather than the ROE. Most repurchases, of shares despite being labelled 'returning capital to shareholders', are really destroying capital for shareholders.

To the extent that you can identify that a business is lacking investment opportunity or that it lacks management talent, you ought to simply avoid that company as an investment.

Some companies accumulate a great deal of cash on their balance sheets. While holding a cash buffer is prudent and so good management, too much cash is a drag on performance.

Cash is an asset and so it is included in the value of assets, equity and capital in our valuation metrics. But cash does not generate a return for the business because it is not being deployed by the business. So to that extent it is a non-performing asset which reduces the ROE, ROA and ROC metrics by increasing the denominator in those equations.

Accordingly, from time to time the company may announce a special dividend whereby it returns excess cash to its shareholders. This is a good thing and a far better use of excess cash than repurchasing shares at over inflated premiums. However, the result will invariably be that ROE, ROA and ROC metrics will improve despite there not necessarily being any material improvement in the business. So be aware and factor this into your analysis.

One additional word of warning. The payment of a strong dividend may be an indicator of a strong company, but this is not always the case.

Some strong companies with reliable steady earnings have a good long term record of paying healthy dividends and are likely to keep on doing so in the future. Examples include the oil giants.

However, some companies appear to pay a high dividend yield because their shares have fallen in price. If the drop in price is due to a decline in the performance or prospects of the company then you may be at risk of losing capital if the shares continue to fall. More particularly the dividend may not be safe – it may be scaled back or abandoned altogether if earnings levels drop further. Said differently, a high dividend can be a warning flag so ensure that you undertake adequate due diligence before investing in high yield companies.

TIMING IS EVERYTHING

Chapter Twenty-Eight

T he million dollar question that most amateur investors ask is how to find great companies in which to invest.

Finding the right company is actually only half the challenge for a great investor. The other qualities required are patience, an analytical mind and a great deal of self-control.

Allow me to tell you an anecdote about three brothers Arthur, Billy and Charles.

These three brothers each inherited $1m at the end of 2007 and they all wanted to invest their new found wealth wisely.

All three of them agreed that Amazon looked like a good prospect with great growth potential.

On 31st December 2007 the market opened with the Amazon shares priced at $90 each.

Arthur and Billy decided that there was no time to waste and so each invested their $1m.

Charles on the other hand conducted some detailed analysis and concluded that although Amazon was a great company, the immediate value of the company was more than covered by the price, which was trading at 82 time earnings and so he refrained from buying at $90. Instead he sat on his $1m cash awaiting a better opportunity.

The share price slowly declined over the course of the next eleven months, helped along by the financial crisis of 2008 and the collapse of Lehman Brothers bank.

On 28th November 2008 Amazon shares opened at $56, traded down to less than $35 and then closed at $42.

Arthur and Billy were concerned about the value of their investment which had halved. Arthur was frozen with indecision and so did nothing. Billy, however, fearing that his investment may fall further in value, decided to sell his shares at a price of $45.

Charlie, on the other hand, saw this as a buying opportunity since he believed that market sentiment had taken the price to a level well below the intrinsic value of the shares. The shares were now trading at a more reasonable 29 times earnings. So he invested his $1m at the same price of $45 per share.

Needless to say, the market recovered and ten months later on 30th September 2009 Amazon shares traded back up at $90.

The lesson to be learned from this story is that all three brothers started with the same sum of $1m, all three managed their assets over the same 21 months period and all three invested in exactly the same company. Yet the outcome could not be more different:

- Charlie's capital had doubled from $1m to $2m.
- Arthur's capital was unchanged at $1m.
- Billy fared the worst and his capital had halved and now stood as $500,000.

And so it is not always the quality of the investment but the timing that makes the difference.

Let us explore timing from a valuation perspective.

At the end of 2007 the Apple shares were showing a PE multiple of almost 40 implying an unattractive 2.5% earnings yield. This was caused by over exuberant investors overpricing the company's shares relative to its earnings, said differently the price did not reflect the intrinsic value of the company. The value to price gap closed over the course of the next six years to the middle of 2013 and the PE multiple diminished to below 10, implying much more attractive 10+% earnings yield.

Why is this important?

If you had bought Apple shares at the end of 2007 you would have paid $24.88 and by the middle of 2013 they would have been worth $50.88. So it would have taken you six years to double your investment – you would have experienced a PE multiple contraction and compounded at 12.66%. Now if you had instead waited until the shares were more attractively priced at the lower multiple you would have paid $50.88 for the shares in the middle of 2013 and my the end of 2019 (a corresponding 6 year period) those shares would have been worth $293.65 a 600% increase – you would have experienced a PE multiple expansion and so compounded at 33.9%.

Why did a 2.5% Earnings Yield in the first period turn into a 12.66% annual return? And why did a 10% Earnings Yield turn into a 33.9% return in the second period? Be reminded that the long term investor enjoys his earnings yield gravitating towards ROE over time. The ROE over the first period increased from 27% to 45% and the 2.5% Earnings Yield was gravitating towards it reaching 12.66% after six years. For the second period the Earnings Yield started at a the higher level of 10% and was gravitating towards a ROE which increased from 29% to 60% over the period reaching 33.9% at year 6.

Again we see that even when investing in a high quality company, timing has an enormous impact on your return on investment.

Nothing more needs to be said on the subject of timing. I feel that the message is abundantly clear.

THE BIG TEST

Chapter Twenty-Nine

Y ou are now nearing the end of this book and so by now you should have a good idea of what to look for in corporate data when looking out for your next investment opportunity.

How confident are you?

Would you like to test yourself against Warren Buffet?

> *NOTE: Whether analysing a single company and comparing year-on-year performance, or analysing one company against another in its peer group, it is enormously helpful to standardise the data so that you are able to compare on a like-for-like basis.*
>
> *The easiest way to standardise is by reference to the top line, namely sales. So, in the examples that follow, we are comparing companies on a like-for-like basis based on a $100 of sales.*

So let us consider two companies on a standard size basis:

	Company A	Company B
Sales	$100	$100
Pre-tax Profit	$1.00	$13.00
After-tax Profit	$0.65	$10.10
Profit margin	0.65%	10.10%

Which opportunity would Warren Buffett select as an investment?

Give yourself a few moments to consider the question before reading on.

I imagine that most readers will select Company B. After all a 10.10% profit margin appears to trump 0.65%.

If you answered Company A then you must be the type that always bets on the under-dog, and probably loses more often than not.

In this instance, for an investor, neither A nor B is the correct answer.

You should have stated that you had insufficient information to make an informed decision. If this was what you were thinking then give yourself a pat on the back.

Investment is largely about return on the money being invested and that information was lacking.

So now we have some more information.

Any idea which company Buffett would choose now?

	Company A	Company B
Sales	$100	$100
Pre-tax Profit	$1.00	$13.00
After-tax Profit	$0.65	$10.10
Profit margin	0.65%	10.10%
Equity (Book Value)	**$6.50**	**$64.10**
ROE	**10.00%**	**15.75%**

You would be in the majority if again you selected Company B. On the face of it a 15.75% ROE is far superior to 10.00%, and you have way more profit per dollar of sales.

It would be difficult to fault your logic. But you still lack sufficient information to make an intelligent investment decision.

ROC is a critically important metric for an investor to consider as it tells you what return the company is generating on its capital. Be reminded that capital is equity, often augmented with debt.

So you need to know the book value (equity) of the company, its debt profile and how much cash it holds (for the purpose of calculating net debt). Finally, knowing the amount of interest being paid on debt allows you to calculate EBIT (earnings before interest and tax) otherwise known as Operating Profit.

Let us look at more data.

So which business do you think Buffett prefers now?

JAMES EMANUEL

	Company A	Company B
Sales	$100	$100
EBIT	$1.00	$15.4
Interest	0	($2.4)
Pre-tax Profit	$1.00	$13.00
After-tax Profit	$0.65	$10.10
Profit margin	0.65%	10.10%
Debt	0	$79.00
Cash	0	$19.10
Equity (Book Value)	$6.50	$64.10
Total Capital	$6.50	$143.10
Debt to Equity ratio	0	1.23
EBIT/Capital	15.40%	10.76%
ROE	10.00%	15.75%
ROC	10.00%	7.06%
ROC net of cash	10.00%	8.14%

We have EBIT, and so we now know the operating profit margin (EBIT/Sales). We are also provided with information pertaining to the leverage of the company and so we are able to calculate the total capital deployed and so, by extension, the ROC.

Does the 15.75% ROE of Company B trump the 10% of Company A?

Does an operating margin of 15.4% for Company B trump the 1% of Company A?

Company B is leveraged, but even after servicing that debt and paying $2.40 of interest, it would appear that the leverage has helped it achieve $13.00 of pre-tax profit from its $100 of sales versus only $1.00 for Company A. And after tax Company B has generated $10.10 of profit versus only 65 cents for Company A.

On this basis you my still have your money on Company B.

Alternatively, you might argue that Company A has a better

EBIT/Capital ratio. It is is generating profit before interest and tax (EBIT) at a rate of 15.4% of capital deployed while Company B is only producing 10.76%.

And although Company B has a ROE of 15.75% versus 10% for Company A, this figure is flattered by the use of debt. When we look at ROC we see that Company A is generating an unleveraged 10% ROC while Company B is only producing 7.06%.

A ROC of only 7.06% for Company B is at the lower end of acceptability based on equity risk premium sought by investors over prevailing risk-free rates. Said differently, there is not very much margin of safety when investing in Company B. In the event of an economic downturn for example, its ROC may drop by 2% moving it under the hurdle rate for a good investment.

By contrast, Company A not only has a margin of safety with a ROC of 10% but it has no debt and so if cash flows come under pressure due to an economic downturn then it has capacity to borrow in order to weather the storm.

The debt to equity ratio of Company B is 1.23 which many would consider uncomfortably high. It has little or no further capacity to borrow should it need to do so.

Company B also requires 22 times as much capital as Company A to generate the same $100 in sales, so it is very capital intensive. Capital Intensity (total capital over sales) is 0.07 for Company A versus 1.43 for Company B.

Said differently, all else being equal Company A may double its sales with another $6.50 of capital, which it could do relatively easily because it has yet to utilise any debt in its business.

By comparison Company B would need to raise a huge $143.10 of capital to double its sales. Having all but exhausted its debt capacity this could be difficult to achieve (unless it issues more shares, 200% more, which would dilute existing shareholders by 66%).

A case could therefore be made for investing in Company A.

So which is the correct answer?

Again, give yourself time to ponder the variables before reading on.

Sorry to keep doing this to you, but yet again we have insufficient information to make an investment decision.

For a value investor we are missing arguably the most critical piece of information – the market price!

> *"The price is an integral part of every complete judgement relating to securities. In the field of common stocks, the danger of paying the wrong price is almost as great as that of buying the wrong issue." Benjamin Graham.*

A good company at a bad price is a poor investment. As we saw earlier in the book, Texas Instruments was a great company at the end of the 1990s, all of its economic data looked outstanding, but it was vastly over-priced and so proved to be a poor investment in the years that followed.

So let us consider the last piece of the puzzle, the price.

	Company A	Company B
Sales	$100	$100
EBIT	$1.00	$15.4
Interest	0	($2.4)
Pre-tax Profit	$1.00	$13.00
After-tax Profit	$0.65	$10.10
Profit margin	0.65%	10.10%
Debt	0	$79.00
Cash	0	$19.10
Equity (Book Value)	$6.50	$64.10
Total Capital	$6.50	$143.10
Debt to Equity ratio	0	1.23
EBIT/Capital	15.40%	10.76%
ROE	10.00%	15.75%
ROC	10.00%	7.06%
ROC net of cash	10.00%	8.14%
Capital Turnover	**15.38**	**0.70**
Capital intensity	**0.07**	**1.43**
Market price	**$6.50**	**$230**
PB multiple	**1**	**3.6**
PS multiple	**0.065**	**2.3**
PE multiple	**10**	**22.8**
Enterprise Value/EBIT	**6.5**	**19**

Now we have a complete picture!

Now which business is the better investment?

The shares of Company A trade at parity to book value and at only a fraction of sales. It has a PE multiple of 10, implying a 10% earnings yield which means that an investor will earn ROE immediately.

By comparison the shares of Company B trades at 2.3 times sales and 3.6 times its book value. Its shares trade on a multiple to earnings of 22.8 which implies an earnings yield of only 4.4% for an investor (generally below the hurdle rate for any value investor)

Remember that the investors initial return in year one is the earnings yield. Only over an extended period of time can the investor expect his return to gravitate towards ROE.

For investors in Company B, starting with a meagre earnings yield 4.5% in its first year, it would take more than a decade before compounded equity growth moves the investors returns to anything close to the 10% available from an investment in Company A today – and that assumes that Company B is still producing a ROE of 15.75% in ten years time!

While Company A only has a 0.65% profit margin, its capital turnover (Sales over Capital) is 22 times greater than that of Company B, resulting in a ROC of 10% for Company A versus only 7.06% for Company B. Remember that metrics such as profit margin must be analysed in context rather than in isolation.

Company A has a very clean balance sheet with no debt, while Company B is heavily leveraged and so may struggle if rates climb or in an economic downturn when earnings drop to a level where servicing debt becomes a problem.

Company A combines high quality with a low price which is exactly what the value investor ought to be looking for.

This was exactly the conclusion that Warren Buffett made – he bought Company A!

Company A is the McLane Company, a wholesale food and non-food distributor, which is now wholly owned by Berkshire Hathaway.

Buffett bought the business for $1.5 billion from Wal-Mart in 2003.

Now being privately owned the company is not available to

trade on the stock-market, and so the price for Company A in our example represents the actual 6.5 times pre-tax income that Berkshire paid Wal-Mart for the entire business in 2003. This provided Berkshire with an initial pre-tax return on capital of 15.4% and an after-tax return of 10%.

As a wholesale distributor, McLane operates on huge volumes and high inventory turnover, coupled with tiny operating and profit margins. Warren Buffett does not chase big profit margins. Return on capital, capital intensity and the capital structure of the business are far more important.

So what is Company B?

Company B, you may be surprised to learn, is not a company at all. It is the aggregate performance of the companies that made up the S&P500 in 2019, formatted as though it were a single business.

This is what passive investors get if they invest in an S&P500 tracker or ETF. Not very good, huh? Worse still, some active fund managers do no better than the underlying index because they invest in the same companies in similar proportions to the index. When the fees and transaction costs of fund managers are taken into account the resultant return is actually worse than the index!

The lessons to be learned here is that passive funds are good for lazy investors but not much else. Active funds should be carefully selected based on the ability of the fund manager, which itself is no easy task. And finally, that if you are prepared to put in the hours, you are more than capable of finding good investments yourself which will outperform the market.

Who needs a magic formula when you have skill and expertise based on a solid understanding of how to analyse public companies?

Of course this example focuses on quantitative analysis only whereas an investor would also look at qualitative factors before investing, but the message that it delivers is loud and clear.

Below is some re-formatted analysis comparing, on a standardised basis, three UK companies operating in the same sector.

		CMC Markets	Plus500	IG Group
		%	%	%
INCOME STATEMENT	Sales	100	100	100
	EBIT	5.9	53.6	39.0
	Net Profit	9.7	35.9	34.2
	Dividends	7.9	27.4	32.2
	Retained Earnings	1.9	8.4	2.0
BALANCE SHEET	Equity (book value)	156.8	80.1	170.1
	Cash	45.5	82.6	82.6
	Debt	1.5	1.6	20.1
	Total Capital (Eqty+Debt)	158.3	81.7	190.2
LEVERAGE RATIOS	Debt/Equity	1.0%	2.0%	11.8%
	Debt/Total Capital	1.0%	2.0%	10.6%
	Debt/EBITDA	13.2%	3.0%	47.4%
PROFITABILITY RATIOS	RNTA	6.4%	44.77%	24.55%
	ROA	3.97%	40.14%	15.10%
	ROE	6.21%	44.77%	20.14%
	ROC	6.15%	43.89%	18.01%
VALUATION METRICS	Market Price	135p	750p	564p
	Retained Earning Ratio	19.03%	23.52%	5.95%
	P/S multiple	3.01	2.31	4.21
	P/B multiple	1.92	2.88	2.47
	P/E multiple	30.97	6.43	12.29
	Earnings yield	3.23%	15.56%	8.14%
	Dividend yield	2.61%	11.90%	7.65%
	Retained earnings yld	0.61%	3.66%	0.48%
	EBIT/Total Capital	0.04	0.66	0.20
	Capital Turnover	0.63	1.22	0.53
	Price to EBITDA multiple	26.11	4.25	9.91
	Profit Margin (Net Margin)	9.7%	35.9%	34.2%

Looking at the simplified Income Statement section we can see that for $100 of sales net profit ranged from $35.9 down to $9.7

Also, while one company retained $8.4 of earnings the other two only retained $1.9 and $2.0 respectively. One company is beginning to stand out from the crowd.

Working down to the Balance Sheet, the stand-out company is only utilising $81.7 of capital to generate $100 of sales, while its competitors require $158 and $190 of capital to generate the same $100 of sales. Were the stand-out company to deploy the same level of capital as its competitors, its top line would double!

The stand-out company also has low leverage ratios with debt only being 2% of the value of its equity.

Moving down further, because of the relatively small amount of capital and debt in the business, the stand-out company has outstanding returns on Net Tangible Assets, on Equity and on Capital.

At the bottom of the table I look at Valuation Metrics. This stand-out company earns far more on total capital deployed and it earns a higher return on equity requiring very little financial leverage. Better still it has a PE multiple of only 6.43 implying an earnings yield of 15.56% which we know will gravitate towards the ROE of 44.77% over time. It is also paying a dividend yield of 11.9% and both the PB multiple and the PS multiple do not look unreasonable relative to its peers.

In the private equity world when companies are acquired valuations are typically calculated on a multiple of EBITDA. Our stand out company is priced in the market at only 4.25x its EBITDA while the other two are more than double that valuation.

The stars are aligned and on 16th March 2020 I add Plus500 Plc shares to my portfolio at a price of 750p. One month later on

15th April 2020, they were trading at 1173p, a 56.4% return on investment. Clearly these shares were under-priced relative to their intrinsic value.

Even after this meteoric rise in price I still feel that the shares are being under-priced. If its PE multiple were to align with that of its peers then its 750p purchase price would need to at least double to 1500p. And so I will hold on to this position choosing to enjoy its continuing earnings power and its healthy dividends. I have no interest in selling to make a fast buck.

Be aware that this side-by-side standard size analysis is one dimensional. It excludes the assessment of growth and all of its aspects (growth rate, growth durability, growth predictability, source of growth and the degree to which it is organic, capital requirements to fuel growth, etc.) As such, this kind of analysis needs to be accompanied by a comparison of the target company's own performance over multiple years so that trends may be analysed – Are sales and earnings increasing, decreasing or stable? Is the company utilising its assets more or less efficiently based on Asset Turnover numbers? Are profit margins expanding or contracting? Is leverage being well managed? And so forth. Without an understanding of the variables affecting growth, an investor cannot assess intrinsic value so cannot gauge whether or not something is a value investment at its current price.

IT'S ALL ABOUT THE MANAGEMENT

Chapter Thirty

M ost of the investment analysis discussed in this book is based around numbers (quantitative analysis). However, it is also important to undertake qualitative analysis.

Some of the qualitative elements that investors seek are subjective. The quality of its management is more objective and is one of the most important aspects of an investment.

When looking at a company's annual reports keep a sceptical mind. Read the notes to the accounts carefully. Remember always that management teams have a perverse incentive to paint over the cracks when it comes to what is essentially an appraisal of their own performance when reporting to the shareholders who employ them.

Benjamin Graham used to classify management into three types:
1. Deceitful;
2. Honest but incompetent; and,
3. Highly proficient.

If he had any reason to suspect that management may fall into the first category he would simply avoid that company rather than taking a chance. Indicators might include the withholding of information from shareholders or evidence of the mismanagement of a conflict of interest – perhaps an unfavourable share repurchase strategy that benefits management by boosting bonuses at the expense of shareholders (think Lou Gerstner at IBM, more on this later); or asset stripping the company and ladening it with high levels of debt to boost short term earnings at the expense of long term prospects (think Philip Green and how he pushed BHS into insolvency).

The second type is also best avoided. These companies will typically have a poor performance record and so are easy to identify. These companies often look to be good value on the surface but they are what is known as a value-trap because their shares are cheap for a good reason. The chances are that shares in these companies will always be poorly priced and so you really want to avoid them as the potential upside is severely curtailed and the risk/reward profile is unfavourable.

Ideally you want to invest in companies with a highly proficient management team which will enhance the business at an attractive growth rate. Ultimately there are three ways in which you will make money from your stock-market investment:

1. Earnings generated by the company which may be paid out as dividends and/or reinvested in the business;
2. Multiple expansion where a company is undervalued at the time of investment but subsequently benefits from a revaluation;
3. The effective allocation of capital by the executives in order to achieve compounded growth for the company in terms of sales, earnings and shareholder equity.

   Only Graham's third category of management will enable you to achieve this.

Distrust future financial projections as predicting the future is difficult if not impossible. It is far better to estimate future earnings potential by assessing the proven past performance of the management team and considering the strength of the business in which they operate.

One of the most important factors to consider is the inherent stability of the business. Benjamin Graham once compared Studebaker, a car manufacturer, with First National Stores, a grocery chain. The grocer made steady and increasing but not spectacular profits, while the car company made big profits but these were cyclical in nature due to the motor industry generally. Graham preferred the grocer as an investment opportunity.

Ultimately, an investment in a company is only as good as the management of that company. After all, the money that you invest in the company is capital that is being managed by other people to produce returns that will hopefully grow the company and so the value of your investment.

How well managements allocate capital is of utmost importance:

- Ask yourself, does the business have the capacity to retain capital and invest it in capacity expansion or other worthwhile projects including mergers and acquisitions.

- Consider whether the company is managed with the prudential use of debt in terms of how much to employ, when to use it and when to pay it down or to refinance it. When it comes to business quality, an easy first test is to look at financial leverage. However, while simple to measure, different businesses can tolerate varying amounts of leverage and it can be sensibly deployed in large size at times. For example, financial institutions such as banks operate with relatively large amounts of leverage due to the nature of their business. However, the general rule is that debt is dangerous. Too many companies will use too much leverage leaving them exposed to unwelcome levels of risk, for example if earnings dip for any reason (perhaps in an economic downturn) or when there is an adverse movement in the cost of debt (interest rate changes or credit rating changes for example.)

- Affordability of debt is something to look at. When a company's debt approaches three times EBIT that makes me feel uncomfortable. Essentially this means that it would take three years of pre-tax earnings to repay the debt. By analogy, consider taking debt in your personal capacity that was three times your annual salary, how uncomfortable would that make you feel? Even when borrowing to buy a property with the use of a mortgage most banks are not comfortable with the risk of lending more than three times earnings and that is with the security of taking the house as collateral.

- The multiple of debt to equity is another useful measure. The company should be seeking to make a return on shareholder equity. That return may be enhanced with a little debt leverage, especially where the return on capital exceeds the cost of capital by a significant margin. Said differently, debt should be used to supplement equity, not to usurp it. I generally like to see the debt/equity multiple below one for this reason. As a side note, if the company has cash reserves then look at the net debt to equity multiple where net debt is the debt less the cash on the balance sheet.

- Other than debt, the other way that a company may raise new finance is through the issuance of new equity.

If the number of shares is increasing then that simply dilutes the equity interests of existing shareholders. Ideally I would like to see that growth can be financed out of operating cash flows and so requires no new equity or debt capital at all.

· Assets need to be maintained and so ideally CAPEX (Capital Expenditure) should always match or exceed the depreciation of assets. Any excess CAPEX ought to represent the financing of growth.

· Dividend policy is usually very telling. If a company pays out most or all of its earnings in the form of dividends then that suggests that it has no opportunity to invest in growth. Paying out dividends is a capital bleed on the company. Good management ought to be able to reinvest earnings to grow the business for the benefit of its shareholders. Looking at it a different way, if you are paid a dividend on a shareholding you will invariably look to reinvest that money somewhere which can be a challenge. And so, if you are invested in a good company which is generating a good return on capital and which is growing at an attractive rate then as an investor you ought to prefer earnings to be reinvested than being paid out in cash. If I were invested in a company producing say 20% return on equity then I would be happy to forgo one dollar of dividends today in the knowledge that it will be worth a dollar and twenty cents next year, a dollar and forty-four cents the year after, and so on! Berkshire Hathaway is a perfect case in point. It is one of the best managed companies anywhere in the world and it does not pay dividends.

· Executive compensation is a great barometer of capital allocation. Is executive pay excessive? How does it compare to compensation of other executives at other companies in the same industry? Is the bonus structure well constructed to properly align the interests of management with those of shareholders?

- Is the management using share buy-backs, write-offs and write-downs of assets or the over-capitalisation of assets to massage short term results in order to qualify for fat bonuses?

- The structure of remuneration ought to be based earnings before interest and tax (EBIT) in order to measure the management performance unadulterated by changes in tax rates or interest rates. In the alternative, a cut in tax rates or interest rates will result in an increase in net earnings and so entitle executives to an increase in bonus payments for increases in earnings for which they deserve no credit.

- Similarly, using metrics like changes in free cash flow can be terrible as motivators because free cash flow numbers can be enhanced by cutting capital expenditures (infrastructure investment) or operating costs (such as advertising) at the expense of the business. Said differently, growth for the benefit of shareholders is sacrificed for short term cash flow enhancements to the benefit of executives seeking a big pay-day.

This is certainly the most difficult part of the equity research.

Big investors such as Mr Buffett have the luxury of being able to meet with the management team of almost any company at which time he is able to conduct a face-to-face interview in order to form an opinion of their ability.

You and I almost certainly do not have that luxury. So what are we to do?

There are four things that you ought to do:

1. Look at the length of tenure of the existing executive team and assess their performance over that time. If the existing management have been together for a decade or more, and over that time the company has prospered, then clearly the team is functioning well and this bodes well for the future. However, if the management team changes frequently, particularly the finance director, then this is a red flag. What is causing people to join and then to leave? Something is not right on the inside. Similarly, if key members of the management team are relatively new and you have no way of assessing their ability then investing is something of a lottery. Warren Buffett has been CEO of Berkshire Hathaway since 1963 and despite being 90 years of age he is not stepping down any time soon!

2. You ought to look to see whether any of the management team themselves own shares in the company other than those shares gifted to them as part of their remuneration package. If the management have confidence in their own ability then they ought to have some *'skin in the game'.* More particularly, if high ranking insiders choose to invest their money elsewhere rather than in the company that they are managing then that ought to be another red flag. Indeed, if we look at the outstanding example of Berkshire Hathaway, Warren Buffett and his wife have 90% of their net worth in the company! More particularly, despite generating revenue beyond almost any other company ($82bn in 2019) and sitting on a cash pile of $128bn, Warren Buffett as CEO and Chairman is paid a modest salary of only $100,000 (yes you read that correctly, one hundred thousand dollars). That is what I call management

interests being aligned with those of shareholders!

> *"In line with Berkshire's owner-orientation, most of our directors have a major portion of their net worth invested in the company. We eat our own cooking... we can guarantee that your financial fortunes will move in lock step with ours for whatever period of time you elect to be our partner. We have no interest in large salaries or options or other means of gaining an "edge" over you. We want to make money only when our partners do and in exactly the same proportion. Moreover, when I do something dumb, I want you to be able to derive some solace from the fact that my financial suffering is proportional to yours."* Warren Buffett

3. You could email the investor relations contact at the company and raise any legitimate queries that you may have as a prospective investor. You should always receive a response. The quality of that response will provide you with a clue as to the quality of the management. If there is no response or else the response is entirely unsatisfactory, then that is certainly a red flag.

4. You should undertake forensic examination of the financial affairs of the company in order to discover whether anything underhanded is going on. On this subject allow me to provide you with an historic case study.

Lou Gerstner is an American businessman, best known for his tenure as chairman and chief executive officer of IBM from April 1993 until 2002. He earned himself a fortune and his net worth was estimated to be $630m at the point of his departure from the company. However, this is what many investors allege that he did:

i. He took on debt to finance share repurchases and to offset dilution from his own stock option program. Balance sheet debt ballooned by $10bn to $29bn leaving the company very leveraged. To make matters worse, almost every dollar of debt was used to repurchase shares and little or none was invested in the business itself. Approximately 25% of the company's shares were bought back during his tenure that resulted in a reduction in the share count by 500m shares to 1.7bn.

ii. A decline in the number of shares as a result of stock repurchases boosted earnings per share (EPS) faster than dollar profits were growing. Most investors failed to notice the difference and blindly took comfort in the EPS growth of 58% As a result, between 1998 and 2001 sales fell consistently yet the share price doubled! This is a perfect example of price and valuation being entirely out of kilter.

iii. Investors also seemingly failed to notice that between 1985 and the end of Gerstner's tenure dividends had halved!

iv. Because shares were being repurchased at a PB multiple above parity he was destroying shareholders equity. As a result ROE appeared to be increasing despite earnings being little changed.

v. The effective tax rate declines due to government tax credits for stock options which provides a further gloss to performance figures by flattering net profit margins, for which he claimed credit, even though gross margins and operating margins for which the management are ultimately responsible remained unchanged

vi. He financed customer purchases of IBM hardware with low interest rate loans while booking 100% of revenues and profits up front.

vii. He disguised debt by moving as much of it as possible off the balance sheet.

viii. In fact he aggressively manipulated accounting and actuarial conventions to inflate reported profits any way he could.

ix. He cut research and development expenditures to push up profits in the short-term.

x. He retired early as a hero before investors realised that the last drop of blood had been extracted from the business long ago.

xi. He then allowed his unsuspecting successor to pay the price for his transgressions which resulted in the board begging for him to return from retirement to "fix" the problems at the company which "he" supposedly ran so well!

I hope that this demonstrates that even the most reputable of companies is not immune from poor management practices.

The problem always stems from a misalignment of the interests of management from those of shareholders.

Ironically, companies often have something known as a Long Term Incentive Plan (LTIP). These are designed, ostensibly, to align the interests of management with those of shareholders. For example, executives are given share options or share grants based on targets which may perhaps be to increase the share price by 50% over the next three years. On the face of it the shareholders in the company ought to be delighted if the share price increases by 50% in 3 years. However, as can be seen from the antics of Mr Gerstner at IBM the means of increasing the share price matters a great deal!

More particularly, these LTIPs are something of a misnomer. An equity investor ought to have a 10 year investment horizon yet these so called "long term incentives" for executives allow the management to reap enormous financial rewards over a relatively short time horizon and then retire leaving their successor (and the shareholders) to pick up the pieces.

There really is no magic formula for how to go about measuring management quality. Measuring accounting integrity is a continuous part of the process. Be on the lookout for aggressive accounting, or red flags meant to embellish performance and/or to enrich executives at the expense of shareholders.

QUALITATIVE ANALYSIS

Chapter Thirty-One

Quantitative analysis, based on numbers, may be performed by any investor on any company. However, qualitative analysis requires an understanding of the industry in which the company operates and the way in which such companies grow and generate returns.

So before you start your analysis ask yourself whether the business that you are considering is within your circle of competence. Are you able to understand it? Are you confident in being able to conduct the requisite research?

> *"Intelligent investing is not complex, though that is far from saying that it is easy. What an investor needs is the ability to correctly evaluate selected businesses. You don't have to be an expert on every company, or even many. You only have to be able to evaluate companies within your circle of competence...The size of that circle is not very important; knowing its boundaries, however, is vital."*
> *Warren Buffett*

If a company is outside of your circle of competence then there is no sense in wasting time. Move on to another company.

If you do feel competent to analyse the company then review annual reports and presentations going back several years. Use a critical eye, take nothing at face value and raise plenty of questions in your own mind.

A non-exhaustive list of the types of questions to which you will want answers is set out below:

Is the business model coherent or is it disjointed and illogical?

Does the company have a good track record of growth and does the company still have room to grow?

Is the business scalable, in other words is there market potential to make significant growth for several years to come?

Has the company duplicated its successes in more than one city to prove that expansion will work?

Or is the company diversifying in such a way that may negatively impact future earnings?

What is the track record of the company in relation to pushing the boundaries of the existing model? (new markets, new products, etc.)

What type of business is it?

Does the company have a competitive edge in its industry or is its market share at risk of being eroded? If the former what is the economic moat that protects the company so that it will still be strong five or ten years from today?

Is it a cyclical business and if so, at what stage of the cycle is the company currently?

Is this a fast-changing industry which may lead to unstable revenue streams?

Does the company have a diversified customer base or is it reliant upon a small number of customers? If the latter, then this presents a clear and obvious risk to future revenue streams as the loss of a single client will have a profound impact. Some healthcare suppliers in the UK, for example, rely on the National Health Service (NHS) for more than 80% of their revenue – if that contract comes to an end so too will the business!

How has the company fared in the past?

Has the company been consistently profitable over the past several years, through good times and bad? If not, do you understand why not? Is there an issue that may re-occur?

Are the growth numbers (particularly revenue and earnings) stable, accelerating or slowing down?

Are the margins (gross margin, operating margin and profit margin) stable, increasing or declining?

How do the margins of the company compare to those of its competitors?

What is being done to improve profit margins?

Is the company able to service its debt obligations?

Is the balance sheet strong?

Is the return on Capital greater than the Cost of Capital?

Is this an asset-light business? If not then you need to understand ongoing capital requirements of the business relative to any depreciation of its assets. It is important to comprehend working capital use and requirements together with prospects for incremental capital investment.

What can you read into the behaviour of the management?

Is there a high turnover amongst the senior management or is it a stable management team? Some of the best companies still have their founders at the helm which is often reassuring. On the other hand, some companies see a high turnover of financial executives which is a major red flag – what are these people seeing on the inside that is causing them to resign?

Are insiders (the management) buying company shares with their own money. Ignore free-shares given as a part of a remuneration package. If the executives have faith in their own ability it would be good to see them investing themselves. If not, why not?

Are the executives acting with integrity?

Is executive remuneration reasonable compared to peers?

Is the share price reasonable?

Does the market valuation, when viewed objectively, make sense ?

Is there a catalyst for the stock price to appreciate?

Is the company a potential take over target due to undervaluation? Be careful with this question because you do not want to invest purely on the basis of speculation about a possible takeover that may never occur. It is merely an ancillary consideration.

Are there any hidden value kickers? For example, if we look at Alphabet Inc, the parent company of Google, it has a vast array of businesses – Google search, Google maps, Google Cloud Platform, YouTube, and its 'Other Bets' collection of yet to be profitable business including Waymo (self driving), Verily (life sciences), Google Fiber and Google Investments – its valuation, some would argue, is less than the sum of the value of the parts. This could open the way for the group to split into separate entities at some point unlocking hidden value for shareholders.

Is the macroeconomic environment favourable? Are there any macro economic risks on the horizon?

Is there any regulatory change or legal change on the horizon that would adversely affect the business? An example is the recent regulatory restrictions imposed globally on the online gambling sector which saw their sales drop and their share prices plummet.

Consider what might happen during the next downturn. If the company revenue declines would costs reduce by a corresponding amount or would cost stay approximately the same? Does the company have enough cash reserves to last several years even if it loses money? How did the company's business fare during previous recessions?

I hope that this chapter provides you with an idea of the mindset that one must adopt when analysing a company.

The management will always desire to paint a rosy picture. Indeed, their future tenure at the helm of the company will depend upon it. So when reading publications of the management team it is of paramount importance that you read between the lines and ask yourself the right questions You are, in essence, being a financial detective.

> *"While it should be emphasized that the overwhelming majority of managements are honest, it must be empha-*

> sized that loose or "purposive" accounting is a highly contagious disease.
>
> "When an enterprise pursues questionable accounting policies, all its securities must be shunned by the investor, no matter how safe or attractive some of them may appear. You cannot make a quantitative deduction to allow for an unscrupulous management; the only way to deal with such situations is to avoid them." Benjamin Graham

Accordingly, do not take annual reports or corporate presentations at face value. Always pry deeper beneath the surface to see what you are able to find.

If you are able to do so, attending the company's Annual General Meeting (AGM) is a great opportunity to hear any issues raised or questions asked by other investors. It will also afford you the opportunity to see how those managing the company respond, which in turn may provide you with a feeling for their competence and integrity.

Do not be afraid to send unanswered questions that you may have to the investor relations team of a company – answering investor questions is what they are paid to do.

The response, or lack thereof, is often very telling. Sometimes you will receive a full and frank response from a senior executive. You may even receive a telephone call from the management team if your question warrants a more detailed response or if the company wish not to respond in writing.

However, if you receive no answer or if a third-party public relations company responds with an attempt to fob you off with a stock-answer then perhaps you ought to move on to consider an alternative investment target!

> *"...we believe in telling you how we think so that you can evaluate not only Berkshire's businesses but also assess our approach to management and capital allocation."* Warren Buffett.
>
> *"Our guideline is to tell you the business facts that we would want to know if our positions were reversed...The CEO who misleads others in public may eventually mislead himself in private...We will always tell you how many strokes we have taken on each hole and never play around with the scorecard."* Warren Buffett.

You may consider this rhetoric to simply be Warren Buffett paying lip service to investors in order to win them over, but you would be very, very wrong. The following anecdote will not only demonstrate his sincerity, but also act as a measure of best practice against which you may measure other CEOs.

In 1996 Berkshire Hathaway created and issued 517,500 class 'B' shares in a public offering aimed at enabling participation in the company by a wider range of investors.

The class 'A' shares were trading at that time at a price of $33,000 each which made them unaffordable for many investors – a 'B' share, representing 1/30 of an 'A' share would be offered at $1,100 per share.

Berkshire Hathaway issued a circular for anyone considering investing in the 'B' shares. Bear in mind that the price of a 'B' share was not something determined by Berkshire Hathaway but instead was calculated mathematically at $1/30^{th}$ of the market price of an 'A' share, and in turn the 'A' shares were priced by the market.

The front page of the 1,396 page circular read as follows:

WARREN BUFFETT, AS BERKSHIRE'S CHAIRMAN, AND CHARLES MUNGER, AS BERKSHIRE'S VICE CHAIRMAN, WANT YOU TO KNOW THE FOLLOWING (AND URGE YOU TO IGNORE ANYONE TELLING YOU THAT THESE STATEMENTS ARE "BOILERPLATE" OR UNIMPORTANT):

1/ Mr. Buffett and Mr. Munger believe that Berkshire's Class A Common Stock is not undervalued at the market price stated above. Neither Mr. Buffett nor Mr. Munger would currently buy Berkshire shares at that price, nor would they recommend that their families or friends do so.

2/ Berkshire's historical rate of growth in per-share book value is NOT indicative of possible future growth. Because of the large size of Berkshire's capital base (approximately $17 billion at December 31, 1995), Berkshire's book value per share cannot increase in the future at a rate even close to its past rate.

3/ In recent years the market price of Berkshire shares has increased at a rate exceeding the growth in per-

---

share intrinsic value. Market over performance of that kind cannot persist indefinitely. Inevitably, there will also occur periods of under-performance, perhaps substantial in degree.

4/ Berkshire has attempted to assess the current demand for Class B shares and has tailored the size of this offering to fully satisfy that demand. Therefore, buyers hoping to capture quick profits are almost certain to be disappointed. Shares should be purchased only by investors who expect to remain holders for many years.

This is the kind of management that you ought to be looking for when you select long term investments.

You may be thinking "Why did Berkshire offer 'B' shares and then seek to discourage investors from buying them?"

In answer to your question, honesty and integrity should not be confused with discouragement. Buffett was managing expectations and inviting people to invest for the long term.

In answer to the question about why issue the 'B' shares at all, in truth Buffett was compelled to do so by his good nature as I shall go on to explain.

Prior to the 'B' share offering, shares in Berkshire Hathaway were unaffordable for many investors (they were trading at $33,000 per share). However, many people wanted to participate in the company's ongoing success. Consequently, enterprising unit trust managers sought to exploit the situation by establishing trusts containing only Berkshire stock – anyone could participate in the unit trust with smaller investment denominations, and the unit trust managers could charge transaction and management fees despite offering no added value.

Warren Buffett refused to allow people wishing to invest in his company to be exploited in this way and so saw the birth of the 'B' shares which entirely thwarted the unit trusts.

However, Buffett knew that buyers of 'B' shares would be smaller investors rather than investment professionals. He knew that they would not necessarily have the skill set to understand the intrinsic value of the company or its shares. And he did not want them to invest blindly, so he offered them the guidance that they would need in the form that you have just read. He told them that his shares were over-priced!

There really is nothing more that I can add on the issue of management integrity!

MACRO-ECONOMIC
CONSIDERATIONS

Chapter Thirty-Two

Other than considering the micro-economics of a company, as most of this book has, an investor must also be mindful of factors in the broader economy that will impact share prices and company performance.

The interest rate environment ought to be one of your primary considerations.

A change in interest rates is magnified. Not only does it have a direct impact on the net profit margins of a company by adjusting the cost of debt, but it also has an indirect impact because it will affect market sentiment in relation to share prices.

This is a topic on which an entire book could be written and a detailed study of macro-economics is beyond the scope of this book. However, I shall attempt to deal briefly with examples of these direct and indirect effects of interest rates.

Consider that lower interest rates will reduce the cost of debt and so will result in a healthier net profit. The opposite is of course also true when interest rates increase.

Interest as a percent of sales averaged about 4% from the early

1990's through to the financial crisis of 2008. After that time we saw a decline in interest rates to almost zero on the short end of the curve, the percentage paid in interest by companies was cut in half, to approximately 2% of sales.

The benefit of record low interest rates has contributed significantly to profit margins in the decade that followed which reached all time highs.

With profit margins of about 10%, 2% of that being due entirely to the lower interest rate environment, you can see that interest rates currently account for one fifth of profit margins. Said differently, if interest rates were to "normalise" and return to pre-crisis levels at 4% of sales then profit margins would correspondingly shrink to 8%.

We know that the profit margin divided by the PS multiple equals the earnings yield. Ergo for the share to offer the same yield after a decline in profit margin, the PS multiple would need to drop by the same magnitude. On the assumption that sales remain constant, the PS multiple will only drop if the price of the share falls – that suggests a 20% price correction.

This result is of course no surprise. We know that the price of a share is the product of its earnings, and so a decline in earnings brought about by an increase in the prevailing interest rates will of course de-value the share.

And this leads nicely on to the indirect effect of an increase in interest rates, namely a change in the sentiment of stock-market investors.

Investors in shares demand a risk premium over a risk-free return that may be achieved on perhaps a government bond. So if you are able to achieve 2% risk free, you might look for 6% from a risky equity – it is a simple risk versus reward balance.

And so, as interest rates rise then so too will the risk free rate which, when added to your risk premium, requires you to seek a bigger return from an equity investment.

The way in which you will achieve a bigger return on an equity investment (return being the earnings yield) is to pay a lower price for the share in the first instance. So a $10 share price with earnings of 50 cents per share yields 5%. If you suddenly demanded an 8% yield you would need to acquire the share for $6.25 based on the same 50 cents of earnings. And so we see how an increase in interest rates reduces the price that buyers are willing to pay for shares in the market.

Now combine the effect of an investor seeking a higher yield with the impact of the reduction in earnings from the affect of the rate hike on profit margins. We have that 50 cents of earnings falling 20% to 40 cents. Now if the market seeks an 8% yield its price for the share falls further to $5. And so, as stated at the beginning of this chapter, a movement in interest rates has an magnified or exaggerated impact on the share price.

Now think about this. Changes in interest rates at lower and lower yields has a larger impact on price.

Why?

Well if we reduce rates by 1% from a prevailing 2% interest rate then we have halved interest rate liabilities. However, if we were to reduce a 10% interest rate by the same 1% then interest rate liabilities are only reduced by one tenth.

The global economy in the second decade of the 21st century has seen record low rates. This means that any change in rates from such a low starting point has a more profound impact on share prices – hence the market volatility seen in 2018 when the US began to increase its rates, thereby depressing share prices, and in 2019 when they reversed that policy, sending stock market indices to new all time highs (the S&P500 was up over 31% in 2019 as a result).

By way of example, in 2019 the 10-year Treasury note (US Government Bond) saw its yield decline from 2.69% to 1.92%, which is a huge 28.6% change (equivalent to the affect of reducing a 10.00% interest rate to 7.14%).

The correlation between interest rates and stock prices is not perfect. It will be interesting to see what happens when lower rates collide with lower growth as the result of the 2020 Coronavirus crisis.

Of course there are a raft of other macro-economic factors to consider other than interest rates. These also include tax rates and money supply as facilitated by central banks. I do not intend to embark on an explanation of how they all affect share prices but instead would like to provide you with food for thought.

In the period from the financial crisis of 2008 to 2020 we experienced a prolonged period of historically low interest rates, money supply expansion through quantitative easing policies and the Trump 2017 corporate tax cut from 35% to 21%.

Any one of these would bolster share prices. It is therefore unsurprising that in combination they resulted in stock-markets reaching dizzying heights despite lacklustre earnings growth over the same period.

With a very few exceptions, the price of equities has run way too far ahead of intrinsic value. It is nothing short of an asset bubble.

Do not be fooled by media hysteria about booming stock-markets. The news providers are in the business of sensationalising everything but understanding nothing when it comes to the world of finance.

It is in fact quite impossible to reconcile a booming stock-market, implying times of economic prosperity, with a reluctance of central banks to increase interest rates from unprecedented low levels due to fears over the fragility of their respective economies. Yet the more the media reports on "another record high for the stock-market" the more money the blind faith investors throw money at it.

No one could have seen the Coronavirus pandemic of 2020 coming, but there was always going to be a catalyst of one kind or another that would bring about a long overdue market price correction.

Warren Buffett generally makes such long term investments that he discounts interim short term peaks and troughs in the economy. However, he does assess the relative value of the market as a whole in macro-economic terms in deciding whether or not the time is right to deploy new capital.

One of his favourite measures of whether or not the market as a whole is overvalued is the market capitalisation of all the companies in the market relative to Gross Domestic Product (GDP).

GDP which enables us to measure the output growth of the economy as a whole. Buffett argues that earnings growth drives intrinsic value growth and that we cannot expect either growth measure to outpace growth in GDP. His position is that while they do not run perfectly in parallel, they are in fact mean reverting over the medium to longer term. When you begin to expect the growth of companies to forever outpace that of the market as a whole, you get into certain mathematical problems.

So it stands to reason that when prices of companies in aggregate (the market capitalisation of the market), runs ahead of GDP, that this is a great indicator that price has in general also run well ahead of intrinsic value.

Let us examine the US market by way of example.

In September 1929, the market cap of all stocks was $93.3 billion while GDP was 103.7 billion – the market cap to GDP ratio was 0.90 which is very high. We all know what happened next - the US stock-market crashed in 1929. By July 1932 the value of shares had fallen 84% while GDP dropped by a more modest 43%. The market cap ratio had fallen from 0.90 to 0.26 – a buying opportunity!

Leap forward to the DotCom bubble of 2000. In March of that year the market cap of all stocks was $14 trillion against GDP of $9.9tn, a ratio of 1.41 – significantly higher than it had been in 1929. Again what followed was a stock-market crash. Share prices halved in the two years to October 2002 but of particular note is that GDP actually increased by just over 10% in the same period. The reason being that most of the overvalued companies were tech companies that were not profitable and were producing no real economic output. In any event the market cap to GDP ratio had corrected from 1.41 to 0.64.

Finally, consider the sub-prime crisis of 2008. The market cap of all shares in October 2007 was $15.9 trillion against GDP of $14.6 trillion. Our ratio was now 1.09. Pop goes the asset price bubble and once again by March 2009 share prices were down 56% while GDP was little changed. The ratio was now a more sustainable 0.49.

Fast forward to the present. By the close of 2019 the market cap of all stocks was 33.8 trillion, propelled by cheap money (interest rates at historic low levels close to zero), the expansion of money supply (otherwise known as quantitative easing – or central banks printing money), and the Donald Trump Tax cuts. GDP was $21.7 trillion which produced an eye-watering ratio result of 1.56! This was undoubtedly a bubble waiting to burst.

At the end of 2019 Warren Buffet's Berkshire Hathaway was sitting on a cash balance of $128 billion. The Sage of Omaha, as he is otherwise known, kept his proverbial powder dry in the knowledge that the market was over-priced and due a correction soon. He had no idea what would bring about the correction, but he knew that after it happened, and he had no doubt that it would, that opportunities to invest his capital at very healthy returns would arise.

The Coronavirus was the catalyst for a correction early in 2020, but if not that we can be sure that something else would have burst this asset price bubble.

The lesson to be learned here is to always be mindful of macroeconomic indicators as they may help you to fine-tune the timing of your investment entry and exit points for new investments.

Alternatively, if you have a portfolio which you are loathed to sell at a time when the market looks ripe for a price correction then you would be wise to hedge your portfolio by investing in downside protection – the derivatives market will assist in this regard but that is a subject for another day and another book!

CONCLUSION

Chapter Thirty-Three

S hort term investing is favoured by some, but long term investing is by far the better approach for building wealth.

If you are looking to hold shares over the longer term then you will need to invest on the same basis that you would if you were buying the entire company outright. In other words you must properly understand the business.

Before investing set out your investment story in no more than two pages explaining, objectively, why you are investing in this particular company.

The explanation needs to be coherent so that anyone else could read it objectively and be convinced by it.

> *"If you can't explain it simply, you don't understand it well enough."* Albert Einstein

This investment story is something that you can refer back to in future in order to refresh your memory and to periodically test whether the investment story stands the test of time.

As a long term investor you will be able to sleep well at night in the knowledge that you have a portfolio of quality companies, regardless of booms and busts in the market.

Price will always tend towards value and whatever the market price from time to time, you will know that the intrinsic value in your portfolio is compounding in your favour.

Good luck with your investing!

APPENDICES

1. <u>APPENDIX ONE</u> - THE MATHEMATICS OF PROBABILITY ASSOCIATED WITH THE GAMES PLAYED BY THE CHEVALIER DE MERE

2. <u>APPENDIX TWO</u> – COMPOUNDED GROWTH PLUS ACCRETION BACK TO FAIR VALUE

3. <u>APPENDIX THREE</u> - THE BETA COEFFICIENT

Appendix One

THE MATHEMATICS OF PROBABILITY ASSOCIATED
WITH THE GAMES PLAYED BY THE CHEVALIER DE MERE

The solution arrived at by Blaise Pascal was the application of
what is now known as the multiplication rule of probability.

In the first game devised by the Chevalier, with a six sided regular die:

$$Probability\ of\ throwing\ a\ six\ with\ one\ throw = \frac{1}{6}$$

Therefore:

$$Probability\ of\ not\ throwing\ a\ six\ with\ one\ throw = \frac{5}{6}$$

And:

$$Probability\ of\ not\ throwing\ a\ six\ with\ four\ throws = \left(\frac{5}{6}\right)^4$$

The probability of throwing at least one six with four throws is the absolute certainty that an event will occur (i.e. a probability of one) less the probability of not throwing a six with four throws:

$$Probability\ of\ at\ least\ one\ six\ with\ four\ throws = 1 - \left(\frac{5}{6}\right)^4$$

= **51.78%**

The probability favours the Chevalier by 3.56% (the difference between 51.78% and 48.22%, the latter being the probability that his opponent would win)

In the second game devised by the Chevalier, applying the same methodology:

$$Probability\ of\ at\ least\ one\ double\ six\ with\ 24\ throws = 1 - \left(\frac{35}{36}\right)^{24}$$

= **49.14%**

This time the probability favoured the Chevalier's opponent by 1.72%.

Had the Chevalier designed the game to involve throwing a double six in 25 throws then his probability of success would have been 50.55%, which is 1.1% in his favour. The smallest margins of error make an enormous difference to success and failure.

Appendix Two

COMPOUNDED GROWTH PLUS ACCRETION BACK TO FAIR VALUE

Over time the price of an investment will compound at a rate equal to the growth rate of the business plus accretion back to fair value.

Imagine a share in a company, the intrinsic value of which you assess to be $10.00 but the market price is only $8.00.

The company is growing at a rate of 11% per annum.

After 1 year the $10 intrinsic value will have grown by 11% to $11.10. If the market price catches up with intrinsic value then you will have seen a 38.75% return on your $8.00 investment (growth plus accretion back to fair value).

The longer that it takes for the market price to catch up with intrinsic value, the less pronounced will be the affect – the accretion uplift is diluted across multiple years.

If it took 5 years, the intrinsic value would be $16.85 which is equivalent to a compounded annual growth rate (CAGR) of 16.1%.

If it took 10 years then the CAGR would be 13.5% and for 20 years it would reduce further to 12.25%.

Either way, buying at a discount to intrinsic value has boosted your return substantially above the 11% growth rate of the company.

Appendix Three

THE BETA COEFFICIENT

In statistical terms, the beta coefficient represents the slope of the line through a regression of data points from an individual stock's returns against those of the market as a whole.

$$\text{Beta coefficient}(\beta) = \frac{\text{Covariance}(R_e, R_m)}{\text{Variance}(R_m)}$$

where:

R_e = the return on an individual stock

R_m = the return on the overall market

Covariance = how changes in a stock's returns are related to changes in the market's returns

Variance = how far the market's data points spread out from their average value

A beta coefficient can measure the volatility of an individual stock in comparison to the volatility of the underlying market.

GLOSSARY

A Non-Exhaustive List Of Some
Of The Terms Used In This Book
That May Not Have Been Defined
In The Body Of The Book

Absolute return

The total return of a portfolio, as opposed to its relative return against a benchmark. It is measured as a gain or loss, and stated as a percentage of a portfolio's total value.

Alpha

Alpha is the difference between a portfolio's return and its benchmark's return after adjusting for the level of risk taken. A positive alpha suggests that a portfolio has delivered a superior return given the risk taken.

Amortisation

Amortisation is the accounting expense associated with the decay of an intangible asset, while depreciation is the same in relation to tangible assets. It should be noted that not all intangible assets decay – consider, for example, the registered trademark Coca-Cola which has arguably increased in value over time.

Balance sheet

A financial statement that summarises a company's assets, liabilities and shareholders' equity at a particular point in time. Each segment gives investors an idea as to what the company owns and owes, as well as the amount invested by shareholders. It is called a balance sheet because of the accounting equation: assets = liabilities + shareholders' equity.

Barriers to entry

Factors hindering the ease of entering of an industry or business area such as high start-up costs, patents, brand loyalty etc.

Bear market

A financial market in which the prices of securities are falling. A generally accepted definition is a fall of 20% or more in an index over at least a two-month period. The opposite of a bull market.

Benchmark

A standard against which a portfolio's performance can be measured. For example, the performance of a UK equity fund may be benchmarked against a market index such as the FTSE 100, which represents the 100 largest companies listed on the London Stock Exchange. A benchmark is often called an index.

Beta

This measures a portfolio's (or security's) relationship with the overall market or any chosen benchmark. The benchmark always has a beta of 1. A portfolio with a beta of 1 means that if the market rises 10%, so should the portfolio. A portfolio with a beta of more than 1 will be expected to move more than the market, but in the same direction. A beta of 0 means the portfolio's returns are not linked at all to the market returns. A negative beta means the investment should move in the opposite direction to the market.

Bid / Offer Spread

A bid/offer spread is the difference between the prices at which you are able to sell and to buy at any given time in the market.

Blue chip stocks

Stocks in a widely known, well-established, and financially stable company, with typically a long record of reliable and stable growth. Usually the companies that are listed in the key benchmark index for the jurisdiction (e.g. FTSE100 companies in the UK).

Bond

A debt security issued by a company or a government, used as a way of raising money. The investor buying the bond is effectively lending money to the issuer of the bond. Bonds offer a return to investors in the form of fixed periodic payments, and the eventual return at maturity of the original money invested – the par value. Because of their fixed periodic interest payments, they are also often called fixed income instruments.

Book value

Value of an asset is its value on a company's balance sheet; this may differ from its market value.

Bull market

A financial market in which the prices of securities are rising, especially over a long time. The opposite of a bear market.

Buy and hold

An investment strategy where a long-term view is taken, regardless of short-term fluctuations in the market.

Capital

When referring to a portfolio, the capital reflects the net asset value of a fund. More broadly, it can be used to refer to the financial value of an amount invested in a company or an investment portfolio.

Capital expenditure

Spending on fixed assets such as buildings, machinery, equipment and vehicles in order to increase the capacity or efficiency of a company.

Deleveraging

A company reducing its borrowing/debt as a proportion of its balance sheet. Within an investment fund, it refers to the fund reducing its level of leverage.

Derivative

A financial instrument for which the price is derived from one or more underlying assets, such as shares, bonds, commodities or currencies. It is a contract between two parties. It does not imply any ownership of the underlying asset(s). Instead, it allows investors to take advantage of price movements in the asset(s). The main types of derivatives are futures and options.

Diversification

A way of spreading risk by mixing different types of assets/asset classes in a portfolio. It is based on the assumption that the prices of the different assets will behave differently in a given scenario. Assets with low correlation should provide the most diversification.

Dividend

A payment made by a company to its shareholders. The amount is variable, and is paid as a portion of the company's profits.

Dividend cover

The ratio of a company's income to its dividend payment. The measure helps indicate how sustainable a company's dividend is.

Dividend payout ratio

The percentage of earnings distributed to shareholders in the form of dividends in a year.

Earnings per share (EPS)

The portion of a company's profit attributable to each share in the company. It is one of the most popular ways for investors to assess a company's profitability.

Earnings Yield

Earnings as a percentage of market price.

EBITDA

Earnings before interest, tax, depreciation and amortisation is a metric used to measure a company's operating performance that excludes how the company's capital is structured (in terms of debt financing, depreciation, and taxes).

Economic cycle

The fluctuation of the economy between expansion (growth) and contraction (recession). It is influenced by many factors including household, government and business spending, trade, technology and central bank policy.

Efficient portfolio management

The idea of investing in a range of assets likely to deliver the best risk-adjusted returns and operate efficiently, ie, to reduce its risk or minimise its costs.

Enterprise Value

Market Capitalisation plus debt less cash.

Equity

A security representing ownership, typically listed on a stock exchange. 'Equities' as an asset class means investments in shares, as opposed to, for instance, bonds. To have 'equity' in a company means to hold shares in that company and therefore have part ownership.

Exchange traded fund (ETF)

A security that tracks an index (such as an index of equities, bonds or commodities). ETFs trade like an equity on a stock exchange and experience price changes as the underlying assets move up and down in price. ETFs typically have higher daily liquidity and lower fees than actively managed funds.

Free cash flow (FCF)

Cash that a company generates after allowing for day-to-day running expenses and capital expenditure. It can then use the cash to make purchases, pay dividends or reduce debt.

Fundamental analysis

The analysis of information that contributes to the valuation of a security, such as a company's earnings or the evaluation of its management team, as well as wider economic factors. This contrasts with technical analysis, which is centred on idiosyncrasies within financial markets, such as detecting seasonal patterns.

Gearing

A measure of a company's leverage that shows how far its operations are funded by lenders versus shareholders. It is a measure of the debt level of a company. Within investment trusts it refers to how much money the trust borrows for investment purposes.

Growth investing

Growth investors search for companies they believe have strong growth potential. Their earnings are expected to grow at an above-average rate compared to the rest of the market, and therefore there is an expectation that their share prices will increase in value. See also value investing.

Hedge

Consists of taking an offsetting position in a related security, allowing risk to be managed. These positions are used to limit or offset the probability of overall loss in a portfolio. Various techniques may be used, including derivatives.

Illiquid assets

Securities that cannot be easily bought or sold in the market. For example, shares with a high market capitalisation are typically liquid as there are often a large number of willing buyers and sellers in the market.

Index

A statistical measure of the change in a securities market. For example, in the US the S&P 500 Index indicates the performance of the largest 500 US companies' shares, and is a common benchmark for equity funds investing in the region. Each index has its own calculation method, usually expressed as a change from a base value.

Leverage

The use of borrowing to increase exposure to an asset/market. This can be done by borrowing cash and using it to buy an asset, or by using financial instruments such as derivatives to simulate the effect of borrowing for further investment in assets.

Liquid assets

Assets that may be converted to cash relatively quickly – including marketable securities, inventory, accounts receivable and of course cash on hand.

Liquidity

The ability to buy or sell a particular security or asset in the market. Assets that can be easily traded in the market (without causing a major price move) are referred to as 'liquid'.

Macro Economics

Macroeconomics is the consideration of the economy as a whole as opposed to considerations at the company level which is Microeconomics. Macroeconomics will include interest rates, GDP, foreign exchange rates, unemployment, etc.

Market capitalisation

The total market value of a company's issued shares. It is calculated by multiplying the number of shares in issue by the current price of the shares. The figure is used to determine a company's size, and is often abbreviated to 'market cap'.

Net asset value (NAV)

The total value of a fund's assets less its liabilities.

Off-balance sheet

Assets or liabilities that do not appear on a company's balance sheet but may be important to assess the financial health of a company.

Passive

An investment approach that tracks an index. It is called passive because it simply seeks to replicate the index. Many exchange traded funds are passive funds. The opposite of active investing.

Portfolio

A grouping of financial assets such as equities, bonds and cash. Also often called a 'fund'.

Position

An investment in a single financial instrument or group of financial instruments, such as a share(s) or bond(s). For example, a portfolio can have a position in a technology company, or through several different shares take a position in the technology sector.

Preference shares

Securities that represent fractional ownership of a company and typically pay a fixed dividend but do not offer voting rights.

Premium

When the market price of a security is thought to be more than its underlying value, it is said to be 'trading at a premium'. Within investment trusts, this is the amount by which the price per share of an investment trust is higher than the value of its underlying net asset value. The opposite of discount.

Price-to-book (P/B) multiple

A financial ratio that is calculated by dividing a company's market value (share price) by the book value of its equity (value of the company's assets on its balance sheet). A P/B value <1 can indicate a potentially undervalued company or a declining business. The higher the P/B ratio, the higher the premium the market is willing to pay for the company above the book (balance sheet) value of its assets.

Price-to-earnings (P/E) multiple

A popular ratio used to value a company's shares. It is calculated by dividing the current share price by its earnings per share. In general, a high P/E ratio indicates that investors expect strong earnings growth in the future, although a (temporary) collapse in earnings can also lead to a high P/E ratio.

Profit margin

Also "Net Margin" is the amount by which sales of a product or service exceeds business and production costs.

Return on equity (ROE)

The amount of income a company generates for shareholders as a percentage of the company's equity that is owned by share-holders. It is a measure of a company's profitability as it shows how much profit a company generates relative to the money shareholders have invested.

Return-on-capital (ROC)

A profitability ratio used to indicate how effective a company is at turning capital into profits.

Risk-adjusted return

Expressing an investment's return through how much risk is in-volved in producing that return.

Risk-free rate

The rate of return of an investment with, theoretically, zero risk. Typically defined as the yield on a three-month US Treasury bill (a short-term money market instrument).

Risk premium

The additional return over cash that an investor expects as compensation from holding an asset that is not risk free. The riskier an asset is deemed to be, the higher its risk premium.

Share buybacks

The repurchase of shares by a company, thereby reducing the number of shares outstanding. This gives existing shareholders a larger percentage ownership of the company. It typically signals the company's optimism about the future and a possible undervaluation of the company's equity.

Shares

See equity. Also commonly called 'stocks'.

Shorting

An agreement to sell something that you do not own at today's price with a view to buying it prior to the delivery date at a lower price. The profit then accrues from the price differential. It is a high risk strategy – if price rises rather than falls then you make a loss and theoretically have unlimited downside risk

Technical analysis

The analysis of esoteric factors such as market liquidity and investor behaviour, and how they influence security prices. This contrasts with fundamental analysis, which looks at factors such as corporate health and the quality of management teams.

Valuation metrics

Metrics used to gauge a company's performance, financial health and expectations for future earnings eg, price to earnings (P/E) ratio and return on equity (ROE).

Value investing

Value investors search for companies that they believe are undervalued by the market, and therefore expect their share price to increase. One of the favoured techniques is to buy companies with low price to earnings (P/E) ratios. See also growth investing.

Value trap

An equity that appears to be cheap due to an attractive valuation metric (such as a low P/E ratio) may attract investors who are looking for a bargain. However, this may turn out to be a 'trap' if the share price does not improve or falls, which may happen if the company or its sector is in trouble, or if there is strong competition, lack of earnings growth or ineffective management.

Volatility

The rate and extent at which the price of a portfolio, security or index, moves up and down. If the price swings up and down with large movements, it has high volatility. If the price moves more slowly and to a lesser extent, it has lower volatility. It is used as a measure of the riskiness of an investment.

Weight Adjusted

Calculations at portfolio level are carried out with inputs that are adjusted according to the size of each holding in the portfolio. So if calculating the beta or volatility of a portfolio, company A which makes up 50% of the portfolio will carry more weight than company B that only accounts for 3% of the portfolio.

Working Capital

Current Assets minus Current Liabilities

Yield

The level of income on a security, typically expressed as a percentage rate. For equities, a common measure is the dividend yield, which divides recent dividend payments for each share by the share price. For a bond, this is calculated as the coupon payment divided by the current bond price.

ACKNOWLEDGEMENT

Reference books and further reading:

Security Analysis, by Benjamin Graham, 1934

The Berkshire Hathaway Inc. "An Owner's Manual" by Warren Buffett, 1996

Market Wizards, by Jack D. Schwager

Berkshire Hathaway annual letters to shareholders from Warren Buffett, 1983-2019

The Intelligent Investor, Benjamin Graham, 1949

One Up on Wall Street, Peter Lynch, 1989

A profile of Warren Buffett appeared in the "Sunday Journal and Star" of Lincoln, Nebraska 1973

Roger Ibbotson's equity risk premium analysis, 1926

Article written by Buffet for Fortune Magazine, 22 November 1999

The Little Book that still beats the Market, Joel Greenblatt, 2006

The Original Turtle Trading Rules, written anonymously by a

Turtle, 2003

The Great Investors, Glen Arnold, 2011

The Pit and the Pendulum, David Harding and James Holmes, 2012

The Warren Buffett Way, Robert Hagstrom, 2013

Common Stocks and Uncommon Profits, Philip Fisher, 2015

ABOUT THE AUTHOR

James Emanuel

James Emanuel qualified in English law. He achieved a Bachelor of Laws degree with Honours and then subsequently secured a post graduate Legal Practice Certificate from the Law Society of England and Wales.

However, having enjoyed the academic side of law, practicing law was not what excited him.

Coming from a family with an aptitude for mathematics and economics - his father, now retired, had enjoyed a career as a stockbroker and his brother practices as an actuary - he was

drawn into the world of banking and finance.

Twenty-five years later, having worked at banking institutions including Citigroup, Deutsche Bank Wealth & Asset Management and Lloyds Banking Group, it was time to document a lifetime of accumulated knowledge for the benefit of others.

During the enforced lockdown of 2020, brought about by the Corona virus known as Covid19, James took the opportunity to write this book.

Printed in Poland
by Amazon Fulfillment
Poland Sp. z o.o., Wrocław